MAKE A NERDY LIVING

MAKE A NERDY LIVING

HOW *to* TURN YOUR PASSIONS INTO PROFIT, *with* ADVICE *from* NERDS AROUND *the* GLOBE

ALEX LANGLEY

STERLING
New York

*FOR KATRINA, WHO MAKES MY
NERDY LIFE WORTH NERDY LIVING*

STERLING
New York

An Imprint of Sterling Publishing Co., Inc.
1166 Avenue of the Americas
New York, NY 10036

ISBN 978-1-4549-3242-0

Distributed in Canada by Sterling Publishing Co., Inc.
c/o Canadian Manda Group, 664 Annette Street
Toronto, Ontario M6S 2C8, Canada
Distributed in the United Kingdom by GMC Distribution Services
Castle Place, 166 High Street, Lewes, East Sussex BN7 1XU, England
Distributed in Australia by NewSouth Books
45 Beach Street, Coogee, NSW 2034, Australia

For information about custom editions, special sales, and premium and
corporate purchases, please contact Sterling Special Sales at 800-805-5489 or
specialsales@sterlingpublishing.com.

Manufactured in Canada

2 4 6 8 10 9 7 5 3 1

sterlingpublishing.com

Interior design by Gavin Motnyk
Cover design by David Ter-Avanesyan
Illustrations by Creees Lee

CONTENTS

INTRODUCTION
THE LIFE YOU'RE LIVING

Like any kid, my idea of growing up involved never *really* growing up. I wanted to keep playing video games 'til dawn, to write something more interesting than the answers to my homework, to make and think and create without having to be interrupted by tasks of the mundane variety. I wanted what we all want—to take what I love and do it for a living.

Today, somehow, I've found a way to do exactly that, and you can, too.

We nerds are passionate when it comes to what we love. Video nerds obsess over putting together cinematic masterpieces or videos of cats reacting to other videos. Crafting nerds obsess over building the perfect props, clothes, gadgets, and gizmos. Writing nerds obsess over making sure every word, every letter, is in exactly the right place to build the perfect story or fanfiction or scathing blog-post review of the newest cinematic chum-bucket. Though making a career out of obsessions such as these used to be a pipe dream, today anyone has the chance to take their passion and make it a profession.

"How can I make a living at this?" is the question many a nerd asks while doing the things they love. *Make a Nerdy Living* is the answer.

This book will explore the myriad ways in which eager nerds can get paid to live their passions and self-start the careers they yearn for. If you've ever watched professional streamers in envy as they rake in cash for playing video games, if you've ever marveled at the skills and artistry of a professional cosplayer, if you've got a half-finished novel or blog post you wish you could complete and get paid for, if you've *ever* hungered to do something a little bit more fulfilling, then this book is for you. *Make a Nerdy Living* is for nerds at every stage in their careers. In these pages are general tips for newcomers, in-depth advice for those with some experience points under their belts, and everything else in between.

Through forbidden arcane rituals, I've melded research, anecdotes, personal experience, and interviews with working nerds to create this frothing tome of intellectual goodness. So if you're bold enough, dear reader, then lock the doors, settle in, and buckle those sweet buns up while I show you some ways you can level up your life and career into the nerdy living you deserve.

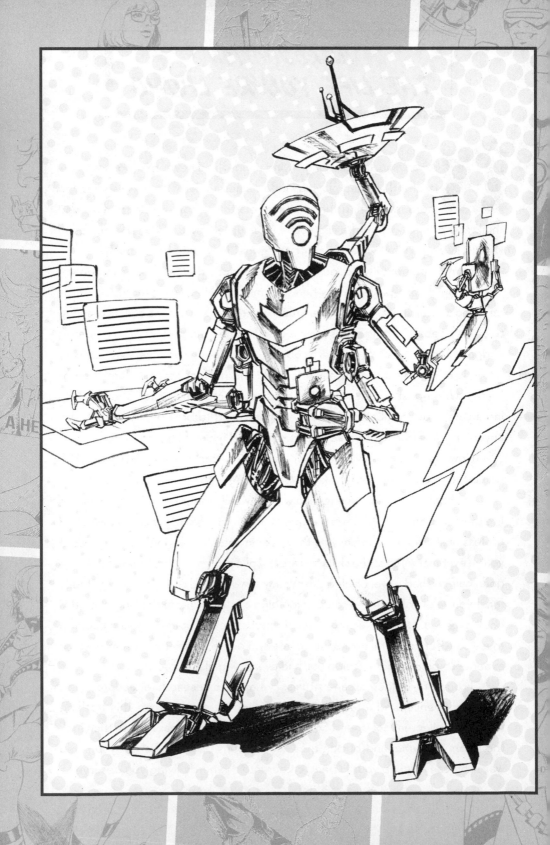

CHAPTER ONE

BLOGGING

Blogs create thoughtful conversations, distribute information, and tell us about the Top Ten Most OMG Moments from *Game of Thrones*. Blogs exist everywhere and cover every topic. Their ubiquitousness and versatility stem from the format's simplicity, requiring only a computer and an Internet connection from both creator and participant. Hence, many folks choose the blog as their first foray into the world of professional nerddom. Blogs are, to put it succinctly, the cybernetic spine running up and down the Internet's titanium endoskeleton.

Though the term is today often used interchangeably with *website*, blogs* are sites that focus on producing content with a personal, conversational voice to it. Sometimes a blog will be laser-focused on a specific individual, like a mom in Detroit writing about the trials and tribulations of raising triplets or a California deep-sea diver discussing the latest gear, techniques, and diving spots. Sometimes a blog will focus on a small group with a theme, such as a band of pun-obsessed chemists or a quintet of would-be *League of Legends* champions climbing its way through the ranks despite the group's chronic halitosis and general suckiness. Sometimes a blog is a whole lotta people posting a whole lotta things vaguely organized around a similar theme, expanding until the theme gets lost and the blog turns generic and grows out of control and we have to call in the US military/Jeff Goldblum to destroy it. Ideally, though, blogs can be about whatever you want—so long as you're honest and passionate and you strive to improve.

---

* In the earliest days of the 'net, blogs were known as *web logs*, until some smart-minded (and lazy) folks decided to abbreviate it.

THE EARLY HISTORY OF BLOGS

In the stone age of the Internet,* blogging took place through platforms such as Usenet, Bulletin Board Systems, and even e-mail lists. As technology advanced and the Internet grew in power and popularity, the rise of forums gave bloggers a platform they could use to reach others. One of the earliest pioneers of blogging was Justin Hall, who created Justin's Links from the Underground. Hall's site offered readers a tour of his life, offering intimate details in a way few had done online, along with a helping of Internet tips 'n' tricks that may seem bizarre and archaic to modern readers.†

Dave Winer, another "forefather of blogging,"¹ created Scripting News, a site described as the "longest-running Web Log on the Internet."² Winer's blog talks tech, movies, social networking—anything and everything on the mind of this forward-thinking entrepreneur. Winer found a readership in his early days by pioneering the relaxed, almost diary-esque, blogging style that is common today.

A few years later, more specialized blogs began to appear. Harry Knowles created Ain't It Cool News, a film-geek site known for its boisterous fanboy-ishness and inside info on the movie biz. After suffering a debilitating accident in 1994, Knowles began finding respite online, joining newsgroups and e-mail newsletters about film gossip, and eventually created the site to act as a home base for all such discussions.‡

Under the nom de plume§ "Belle de Jour," Dr. Brooke Magnanti created Diary of a London Call Girl, a blog chronicling the time she spent as a high-end escort after she submitted her PhD thesis in forensic pathology. Thanks to her smart writing and the salacious mystery behind her true identity, Dr. Magnanti's blog exploded in popularity. Since then, she has gone on to become a respected academic, authoring numerous books on science and sex, and inspiring the television series Secret Diary of a Call Girl.³

---

* Aka the '80s and early '90s.
† Bonus points to those of you who know what hypertext servers or MacHTTP are. Your '90s-fu is stronger than mine.
‡ Throughout the book I will be referencing numerous Internet peoples, some of whom are cool and some of whom only seem cool at the time of my writing and later turn out to be secret Nazis or butt-grabbing creeps or something. If such an event should occur, know I don't approve of Naziness or creepy butt-fondlage, and you shouldn't, either.
§ A fancy, French way of saying pen name, but also a term for the pseudonym some writers will use.

In 1993, scientist and skeptic Phil Plait established Bad Astronomy to clear up common misconceptions and myths about the science of all things spacey.* Plait breaks down the science of things such as the ill-likelihood of a Planet X cataclysm wiping out life on Earth, why equinoxes and solstices have no special power over eggs, and why the moon landing "hoax" is wrong, wrong, *wrong.* Thanks, in no small part, to his blog, Phil has appeared on shows like *The Late Late Show with Craig Ferguson, Penn & Teller's BS!,* and *Crash Course Astronomy;* he's also netted book deals and become a staple contributor to several websites in need of someone with a healthy dose of brains and skepticism.

Bethany Keeley's *"Blog" of "Unnecessary" Quotation Marks* achieved fame through its simple premise: pictures of signs with "quotation" marks that are not "only" unnecessary but often "imply" the opposite of what the presumed writers were "trying" to "imply."[4] The site is a little less article-focused than most blogs, illustrating the flexibility of blogs as a medium.

MY GOD, IT'S GETTING BIGGER

As the millennium neared its end, blogs' popularity exploded with the force of a thousand flying-toaster screensavers. Geocities, Open Diary, Live Journal, and even MySpace made it easier than ever for the not-so-tech-savvy to get their voices heard. Today, blogs are *everywhere.* Anyone with an inclination toward writing tends to have one, even if it's merely as a supplement to their true passion of doing webcomics, painting ceramic mugs that look like *Star Wars* characters, or posting long-winded video essays about *My Little Pony.*

Creating a web log is easier than ever before, whether you're the most cybernetically enhanced futurist or a grandparent who doesn't know their ISP from their ASS. This is a double-edged sword† for blogging hopefuls, however, as the path to blogging success is much more crowded than it was a scant handful of years ago. Don't despair, dear reader! For you have an edge on the posers and wannabes—you've got enough determination to make a nerdy living that you're now reading a book on *how* to make a nerdy living.

---

* Except for Kevin Spacey.
† Aren't most swords double-edged? Why don't we just assume swords are double-edged unless we clarify they're not?

STARTING POINT: BLOGGING

A blog is arguably the easiest career to start among the many mentioned in this book. Your supply list is pretty straightforward:

- Access to a computer
- Access to the Internet
- A hosting platform, i.e., the virtual landlord to the virtual lot on which you'll build your blog

That's it! Blogging is so accessible, it can be done for free, through publicly available computers at your local library, on a free hosting platform. It's not *recommended* you do that, however, as public computers are a trifle insecure, both in terms of password safety and their emotional states, and the last thing you want is for your burgeoning blog to get taken over by Russian hackers or your computer rambling about its mommy issues.

So, if possible, keep the blogging at home. If your computer's old, no biggie. It doesn't take a lot of computer power to get a blog chugging along, so grab a keyboard and get to clacking!

PICK A PREMISE

Your blog can be about whatever you want—no matter how niche it may seem, there will be others with the same niche interest. After you've chosen a topic, don't feel like you've sold your soul to a dark deity and bound yourself to said subject for the rest of your life.* If you start off with a fantasy-sports blog and find yourself talking more about games in general than fantasy sports, that's fine.

Conversely, fully abandoning your primary premise comes at a cost. If you start a blog about meat-smoking techniques, then begin filling it with more and more rambling posts about the state of British politics, you're likely to drive your current readers off. Try to find a way to naturally integrate your evolving tastes into your current format without abandoning your primary

---

* Unless your topic is selling your soul to dark deities, in which case, yeah, your hands are pretty tied.

premise. However, if you really and truly know your heart isn't into your original premise anymore, you may want to get the potential hit in readership over with and swap topics now before the *sunk cost fallacy** drags you in too deep. Blogs with broader focuses will likely have a harder time drawing in initial crowds but easier times during these kinds of transitions, so keep that in mind.

FOCUS AND DIVERSIFY

Next, decide whether you want your blog to be your main focus or a supplement to the thing you're actually trying to do—and it's okay to change your mind later on! There are plenty of people who start a blog as a companion to their YouTube channel only to find far more readers flocking to their writing than to their videos. Make your nerdy living however you want, and don't limit yourself to trying to make it just one way. While the Paris Hilton/Nicole Richie reality series *The Simple Life* wasn't exactly loved by the critics, it made enough money that Fox felt comfortable making three seasons of *Arrested Development*, which was critically beloved but didn't manage to reach a broad audience in its initial run. If your videos are helping you gain traction online, keep at them even if the thing you're most interested in is writing your blog (or vice versa). Once you've established a foothold online, you will have more flexibility toward building the career you want.

RESIST THE DARK CALL OF CONTENT THEFT

It starts out innocuously enough. At first, you've got a gaming blog with rich, detailed articles full of witticisms and analyses. Then, as you grow busier, you start supplementing the site with listicles full of Top Tens and the like. You try to make your titles clear and straightforward, but after a cleverly misleading title gets you some extra hits, you find yourself leaning more and more on titles like "Princess Peach Is Pregnant—and You Won't Believe Who the Dad Is!" or "Get Ready for the Feels, True Believers, With This Amazing Gamer Proposal!" or "Your Puny Human Mind Will Melt When Trying to Comprehend the Cuteness

---

* The *sunk cost fallacy* refers to the tendency to continue doing something that isn't worth your time, effort, and resources because you've invested so much into it you feel like you simply *can't* switch.

of These 22 Pikachu Pics!" Then you're adding in slideshows full of gaming memes and articles that are just screencaps of other people's tweets about games, and pretty soon you're not actually writing anything, merely copying and pasting other people's material and taking credit for it. Your beautiful gaming blog is a gaming blog no more; it's a digital van of stolen goods and you're the creep in an Iron Maiden T-shirt trying to sell to middle-schoolers.

Plagiarism is a real thing, people, and it's one of the worst offenses a writer can commit. Stealing someone else's material, whether maliciously or not, is just that—*stealing*. We writers live by our words, and when you take those words, you're taking someone else's livelihood. The Internet may be a little bit Wild West when it comes to plagiarism and copyright; you still shouldn't go black hat and take what you please. A single plagiarization now could cost you the job of your dreams in the future.

ALSO RESIST THE DARK CALL OF TOPIC HOMOGENIZATION

It's all too easy to let your blog become a sprawling thing devoid of any real content. Video-game blog Kotaku may post a wide variety of articles, but they generally tie back to the over-arcing topic of video games. At the other end of the spectrum we have College Humor, a site once devoted to the art of comedy (generally with a college-oriented twist to it), which is now a generic news site full of articles like "Seven Shows Where the Main Character Is the Worst Character"[5] and "Five Love Songs Not Actually About Love."[6] Both humor and college have long since left the haunted ruins of that once-mirthful site. It's not alone—other sites have been desiccated down into zombified shells of potential entertainment because of the corruptive touch of topic homogenization. Never lose focus on the true essence of your site, whatever it might be.

PICK A GOOD WEB ADDRESS

ChloeMatthewsWorldOfCatsAndCrochet.com is a descriptive URL. It's also as long as hell and no one is going to remember it. Brevity is the soul of wit[7] and the soul of web addresses. ChloeCrochetsCats.com makes for a far pithier address while giving a cheeky hint as to what your site is about. The easier a URL is to remember, the easier it will be for people to remember to visit.

BLOG RESPONSIBLY

As the Internet has expanded, the battle for the ever-elusive clicks has grown fiercer. Two issues that became epidemic problems circa 2010 were clickbait and journalistic integrity.

Clickbait refers to deliberately attention-grabbing, often misleading article titles that are more focused on getting people to click the article and generate ad revenue than in providing information of substance. This technique originated in print journalism; the clickbait of decades past was referred to as *yellow journalism* and used the same techniques as modern clickbait to exploit curiosity. Tabloids used it to a humorous intent with stories like "Garden of Eden Found!" or "Elvis is Alive—and Running for President!" or "Bat Boy Leads Cops on 3-State Chase!"[8] Others created sensationalistic headlines about celebrities, politics, and health, trying to badger readers into picking up a copy by using their fears and curiosity against them.

While the format has changed, the tactics haven't. Today's journalists are in a faster race than ever to be the first to post big news, and things like journalistic integrity can get left by the wayside. Thanks to the Internet's instantaneous information-spreading powers, the time it takes for a story to break and to become old news is virtually nil. In the race to be the first, many writers don't have time to check facts or sources, instead contenting themselves to course-correct misinformation with nothing more than the word *update* added to the headline and a blurb at the bottom of their article explaining the whole thing was false. Others don't even go that far, counting on the rabble of the Internet to wash over the fact they were wrong.

If you want to become a professional blogger, the urge to clickbait and write without fact-checking may gnaw at you from time to time. Be better. It's fine to write attention-catching headlines; connect them to articles of substance and don't trick people into clicking to up your number of views. Do your best to get the scoop on news while checking with multiple sources before posting unless you've got a direct source—e.g., you're the first to post about the new Spider-Man re-re-re-reboot because you have an archived video clip of Stan Lee talking about his cameo as Unus the Untouchable's cousin, Anus the Antagonistic.

USE A PSEUDONYM IF YOU WANT

Some bloggers choose to use pseudonyms; others don't. The choice is entirely up to you. The Internet can be a fun place. It can also be a scary, unforgiving place full of stalkers and hackers. If you're planning on blogging about incendiary topics such as politics, racial strife, or which MST3K host is the best,* using a *pseudonym* (literally, "fake name") may help save you from some pain down the line. If you do, claim your pen name across every social media platform to ensure uniformity for your brand.

CHOOSE A SOLID HOSTING SERVICE

You, lucky reader, have countless blog platforms at your fingertips. Some people run their blogs through free sites such as Tumblr®, which sacrifices customization power for ease of access and low cost, or with blog tools like WordPress®, which meet a happy medium between user-friendliness and adaptability.† Subscription-based monthly services vary in quality while generally offering more bang for your buck (since you're actually spending some bucks). You'll want a service that won't severely limit your data or throttle your site if and when traffic gets too high—there's nothing worse than having your first big viral post lose momentum because your stupid provider is throttling your traffic to slow down the tide and keep their costs low.

MAKE AN E-MAIL ADDRESS FOR BLOGGING AND
GET ON SOME PRESS LISTS

Whatever it is you're going to talk about, you'll need some fodder for discussion. Press lists are direct connections to studios and other news sources, offering press releases and review copies for journalists. Subscribing to the right press list helps you get on the front line of the hottest news, so whether you're gabbing 'bout games, chatting 'bout cats, or talking 'bout tanks, subscribe to as much press-related stuff as you can. Plus being on press lists ups the odds that you can go to conventions with *gratis* press passes.

---

* The correct answer is, of course, Captain Picard.
† If you're reading this in the future, Tumblr and WordPress may not still be around. If so, just mentally replace them with similar services, and also try to send me a message back in time to let me know whether or not I should invest in those alpaca farms.

THE NEXT STEP: BLOGGING

The early days of blogging are unfettered and carefree. You spend your moments blissfully spilling your thoughts onto the Internet, unconcerned about pesky things like grammar and audience. As you continue blogging, however, you'll want to hone your professional edge. You'll need to stop treating blogging as a hobby and start treating it as a job. A job you're not getting paid for yet, but a job nonetheless.

REDECORATE OCCASIONALLY

Website layout is a constantly evolving beast, sprouting wings and gills and laser eyes as needed. In the late '90s, blogs' front pages had numerous links containing tons of sub-areas to scour and explore. Back then, readers liked that sort of thing; the Internet was so new to most of us, we relished exploring it like a *D&D* party scouring every nook and cranny of a dungeon.

In the mid-2000s, it became en vogue for websites to splatter every single thing you could possibly need on the front page, minimizing the number of clicks you needed but also increasing information overload. Around 2010, sites began shifting to a more vertical layout to fit the confines of a phone screen. Despite its early successes, Harry Knowles's Ain't It Cool began to languish in part due to the site's refusal to evolve its layout beyond an early-2000s information vomit.

So how should you lay out your blog? Your best bet is to analyze the layouts of your favorite sites and think about what you do and don't like about them and why they made the choices they did. Ask your friends and family to test out your site and give you feedback.* Whatever you choose, you're not locked in, so change it up as needed.

FOCUS YOUR VOICE

Newbie fiction and nonfiction writers will often make the mistake of thinking readers will be interested in their main character because they're the *main* character. Nope. Readers will only be interested in a main character if they

---

* Friends and family—our invaluable, infinite guinea pigs.

can find some way to connect to them. As the primary voice behind your blog, you're the main character, which means you need to interest the audience. Banal stories of everyday occurrences aren't going to cut it. If you want to keep people interested, you'll need to find a way to set your blog—your voice—apart from the rest of the Internet.

For some bloggers, they're different because their writing is laser-focused on something niche and specific. For others, it's not so much the subject that will draw people in as the unique perspective of the author, so whether you're a myopic English major or a black lesbian anime fan or a professional-chef-turned-real-estate-mogul-turned-vampire, employ that to enrich your writing. If all else fails, let the quality of your wordcraft be the thing differentiating you from the competition.

FLOW

We pursue these nerdy careers, as ethereal as they may feel sometimes, because they're what grant us *flow*, the state of being one with an activity, of losing yourself to the stimulating work before you, becoming unconcerned with everything except the sheer pleasure of creating.

In their article "Flow Theory and Research" in *The Oxford Handbook of Positive Psychology*, psychologists Nakamura and Csíkszentmihályi[9] break flow down into its constituent factors. Flow provides an intense concentration on the present moment, a merging of action and self-awareness, a loss of hindering self-consciousness, a sense of control, a sense of reward, and a loss of awareness of the world outside your task. To put it scientifically, flow is a really rad feeling of getting shit done that leaves you super-satisfied.

The question is: How do you achieve flow?

DETACH YOURSELF FROM THE PHYSICAL AND ELECTRONIC WORLDS. This may sound a bit zen-buddha-Jedi, but we live in a far more distracted world than the creatives of decades past. Andy Warhol didn't have to worry about texts and social media notifications pinging his phone while he was working because they didn't exist in his heyday. If you really want to flow, put your phone into DO NOT DISTURB mode and let the people in your life know to leave you alone for a few hours.

Doing this also requires you to give yourself permission to detach from everything else and immerse yourself in the present moment. This means getting your mind in a state where you're comfortable not answering messages or dealing with daily problems. This can be achieved through force of will, but it also helps if you deal with the little things before you get started so they don't nag at you while you're trying to dive into your work.

TAKE SMART BREAKS WHEN NEEDED. getting up and walking around/stretching the muscles every hour or so is a good idea, as it keeps the blood flowing and will prevent you from dying from a blood clot—a death more common amongst nerdy types than you might think! Whether you're pausing to stretch your legs, get a drink, or go to the bathroom, do not bring your phone with you. Lots of people like to quickly check Facebook or get in a round of their favorite time-killing game when taking a breather, which is a bad idea. Such distractions crack your flow open and leave its flow-blood flowing everywhere. Just because your fingers aren't working doesn't mean your mind isn't, so let your brain keep doing its thing while you stretch out those muscle fibers.

SET GOALS. Whether it's a specific word count, a specific page colored in your comic, or a specific piece of your Tyrion Lannister statue whittled into shape, some people work best with a finish line in mind. Of course, other creatives will do great work yet slow themselves down with worries about not getting "enough" done for the time spent. Good work is good work; there's no pre-determined amount of progress you should be making for the amount of time spent on your project. Figure out whether you prefer set goals or if you're the type to sweat these sorts of things, and adjust your work style accordingly.

FLOW WILL BE ELUSIVE AT FIRST. As you're first starting out, achieving flow will be difficult, and, at times, impossible, because the actions you need to take aren't yet automatic. Be patient. Continue practicing, and eventually you'll realize you've been flowing without realizing it.

BE MOTIVATED BY THE RIGHT THINGS. As Yoda said in *The Empire Strikes Back*, "Adventure. Excitement. A Jedi craves not these things." Motivation, our reason for doing the things we do, comes in two flavors: *extrinsic* and *intrinsic*. Extrinsic motivation refers to being motivated by external rewards like fame and fortune. Intrinsic motivation refers to doing something because the action of doing said thing is rewarding in and of itself. We work jobs we don't like because they pay the bills; we work jobs we love, even when they don't pay the bills, because we *love* them. Extrinsic motivation is fine for the more basic things; but if you're going to make a nerdy living, you need to be in it because you love what you're doing, not because you have some ulterior goal in mind. If you try to write books because you want to be a famous author, you will fail. You have to write books because you find the task itself intrinsically rewarding.

Intrinsic motivation is by far the more powerful motivational force; there are countless people who keep working and practicing the things they love even if they're not being paid to do it simply because they love to do it. Before you expend the resources toward making a nerdy living, take stock of why, exactly, you want to make a nerdy living and make sure they're reasons that will keep you motivated in the days, weeks, and even years to come when the only thing motivating you is *you*.

RELISH YOUR PROGRESS. Striving to perform and create better is a good thing. At the same time, you need to take a moment to allow yourself the feeling of reward that comes with making progress. Some days, you won't feel as if you've made much progress. Others, you may feel as if you're moving backward or undoing previous progress. These days still provide valuable experience that makes you better at creating, so try to focus on the overall positive instead of the momentary negative.

Ultimately, though, it's important to understand FLOW IS DIFFERENT FOR EVERYONE. My brother-from-another-mother Marko Head, for example, finds his flow drawing with television shows or podcasts playing in the background. I, on the other hand, have trouble getting my writing flowing if there's another person in the room, let alone if there's someone talking through a headset or on a small screen, which is one of the reasons I listen almost exclusively to video game soundtracks and video game-inspired music while I work.* As you work more and more, you'll find what your flow is, so don't let anyone tell you your way is "wrong" and theirs is "right." If you're getting the work done, if you're flowing, and as long as your flow doesn't involve hurting anyone through blood sacrifices and the like, then your flow is the right kind of flow.

But, before you get to flowing, you'll need to find whatever activity (or activities) which flow your bow, so keep reading to figure out what exactly that may be.

SELF-IMPROVEMENT NEVER STOPS

Sucking at something is the first step toward becoming kinda good at something.[10] After you've been blogging for a while, you're probably going to look back at your earliest writing and cringe. Good. You *should*. If you don't, it means you haven't improved and are deluding yourself about the quality of your writing (we all have trouble seeing our own shortcomings sometimes). No matter what you're passionate about doing, you must have an equal amount of passion for growing better at it. Those who don't will become—at best—hacks with limited audience, and at worst, will achieve nothing. If you want to edge out the competition, turn a critical eye inward to see what you can improve about your writing.

---

* With the other reason obviously being I am a super-cool dude.

BASIC GRAMMAR TIPS ALL BLOGGERS SHOULD KNOW*†

- Use spellcheck. You have a magic machine capable of pointing out when you've spelled something wrong, but you didn't use it and now your most popular blog post is called "Top Five Tips for Making Healthy Fruit Smoo"? For *shame!* Go stand in the corner for a minute and think about what you've done, then come back and use your damn spellcheck.

- Effect is a noun, affect is a verb. Something has an effect, and you are affected by it. Do not mix these up.‡

- There, their, and they're. They're not the same, so know their different meanings and use them here and there as needed.§

- Semicolons, colons, commas, and periods are all different and do different things. If you think you need a semicolon, odds are high that you don't. Commas denote a series of things in a list or join independent clauses, colons denote that the clause following it is a list, and a semicolon connects two closely related clauses. That's right, fool, we're talkin' 'bout clauses! It's not all fun and games being a nerdy pro!

- Know your tenses. Whether your tense is past, present, or future, perfect or imperfect, keep it straight in your writing.

- Capitalize the first words of sentences; proper nouns such as people, places, and things; as well as most words in headlines except for small articles like *a*, *an*, or *the*. Also capitalize commonly abbreviated phrases such as OMG, AFK, or ROTFLUMSBAIHTGTTHWIMMTWGSABATTOUEUOASSIM.¶

---

* "B-b-but my favorite writer doesn't follow all these rules all the time!" Yep, but I'll bet my bodacious buns your favorite writer *knows* these protocols so they can choose to break them at the right moment, rather than indiscriminately, unwittingly shattering the rules.

† These tips are all based on American grammar, which is different from British grammar in that the rules are slightly tweaked and it's 42 percent less fancy.

‡ I see you over there, thinking of mixing them up. Don't you *dare*.

§ Same goes for *your* and *you're*.

¶ "Oh my god," "away from keyboard," and "rolling on the floor laughing until my spleen bursts and I have to go to the hospital where I meet my twin who got separated at birth and the two of us end up opening a surf shop in Maui," respectively.

- **Stiff writing isn't necessarily formal**, nor is it good. Don't write every post like you're trying to get an A on an English paper. Contractions are fine. Write conversationally without getting so loose that it becomes unfocused.

- **I once heard someone say** stream-of-consciousness writing was an avant-garde means of expression outside a theater—not the movie theater, mind you, but the actual theater where actors perform live plays in front of an audience, which I realize now must be really tough because of the distraction of phones, like, you're up there performing and you see phones lighting up the bored faces in the audience, or maybe they're not even bored, they just really need to check their e-mail to see whether or not the alpaca farm they invested in is going to make any money before the end of the month because your wife is going to absolutely destroy you when she finds out you emptied out your savings because you were positive it was a sure thing, which reminds me . . . What was I saying? Oh yeah— stream-of-consciousness babbling is probably a bad idea.

- **Do some research.** This section only covers some of the basics. As you practice your writing more and more, brush up on grammar and keep your skills up to snuff, lest you run the risk of sounding like a mush-mouthed sewer-dweller.

STICK TO A SCHEDULE (BUT TAKE A BREAK IF YOU NEED ONE)

Whether you update your site once a week or once a day, find the groove that works for you, stick with it, and notify readers what that groove is. As a reader, few things are as annoying as finding a great new site only to have it update unpredictably. Random updates lead to sparse readership. If possible, try to plan ahead and create a buffer of several posts so, should you get sick, get busy, or get plain ol' burnt out, you'll keep the content flowing while you're AFK.

USE WHAT YOU KNOW

If you have an advanced degree or specialized interest, don't be afraid to incorporate the perspective that knowledge brings into your writing, even if it's a bit off-topic. For example, if you have a degree in computer engineering and blog about video games, add a paragraph or two to each article hitting your topic du jour from the computer-engineering angle. If you're a zombie running a movie-review site, you could add in a rating system in each review analyzing how tasty-looking those humans are or whether any zombies were mistreated in the making of the film.

You could also work to become a self-made expert in something esoteric, like a particular style of film, video game, or Little Debbie's snack cakes.

INTERACT WITH READERS WITHOUT SEEMING DESPERATE

Answering questions people post after your article? Good! Thanking people who post particularly kind or personal comments? Good! Commenting on the comments of every single person who responds to your post, and then commenting on *those* comments? Less good. In fact, kinda bad. It makes you seem desperate and can make pedantic readers expect unreasonable amounts of interaction from you when you don't have the time for it. Answer questions, comment on other people's blogs, and try to write posts that foster intelligent discussion by integrating open-ended questions to encourage people to respond (try to add better questions than the over-used "What do you guys think?").

BE CAREFUL WHEN GIVING ADVICE

If you plan on running any kind of advice column, be *careful*. There's a reason psychologists have to go to a lot of school to do what they do, and it's because advising people on their lives is something that must be done with intelligence and discretion. Advice columns, in general, are kind of a bad idea, as they frequently have untrained people giving their thoughts on situations they don't have complete information about. If this type of blogging is something you feel passionately about doing, then take it seriously, get the right training, and don't give advice you're not fully sure of.

ENCOURAGE READERS TO KEEP IN TOUCH

To help encourage repeat readers, encourage your audience to subscribe via RSS feed or e-mail. These may seem a bit antiquated to some, but they're solid ways to let interested people know when you have new content. Also encourage them to follow you on other social media platforms by having unobtrusive links to your various profiles at the end of every article.

MAKE FRIENDS

Blogging can be a lonely profession, and since many blogs are one-person operations, the pressure to succeed can feel almost overwhelming. To let some steam out of your mechanisms before you go kablooey, try to build up a network of people you can depend on. Find other blogs discussing similar topics and reach out to their writers to see if they'd like to do a guest post for you. Do guest posts for them. Collaborate together on an überpost. Do whatever you can to connect with your fellow bloggers—it's good for your business, and it's nice to make friends.

WORDS FROM WORKING NERDS

Jenna Busch, writer, journalist, blogger, editor-in-chief, host, geek personality (if properly caffeinated), and public speaker

I was a makeup artist in Los Angeles, which started as a job to support my acting habit back in New York City. I left acting and was traveling as a global artist for a makeup line. One day my buddy and old theater crony from high school, Chris Radtke, called me and asked if I wanted to interview Jack Nicholson and Morgan Freeman for a movie for his website. You don't say no to that. I started working for [pop culture–comedy site] UGO.com, reviewing, and then covering, video games, TV, and comics as well. Once I did a few things on camera, I was asked to appear on shows, and the rest is very geeky history.

What's your daily routine like?

There really isn't an average workday for me. Some days I sit in my pajamas and write news stories for websites—sometimes over 10,000 words a day. Some days I interview celebrities for a movie on camera and then head overseas for a visit to a movie set. Some days I spend on a red carpet in a cocktail dress and slippers (the camera only sees you from the waist up). Sometimes I run around conventions moderating and appearing on panels. The only thing I don't do is sleep.

What has surprised me the most [about the job] is how little journalists are actually paid. It's gotten worse over the years. People often think that because we sometimes interview celebrities, we must be paid like them. I do get to go on amazing trips and do fun things, but I'm still scrambling for work like everyone else. The other thing that surprised me was the number of hours that go into what journalists do. You can't really have a life or make plans, because something always comes up last-minute. I've been sent out of the country with two days' notice, [and I've been] called in to cover a film with less than an hour['s notice]. I've logged 25,000 steps a day at conventions, doing eleven panels and writing about thirty more. There's no "we'll meet up for lunch next week."

What barriers have you had to overcome to get where you are?

I've had to overcome the fact that there were no other women covering geek entertainment when I started. I can't even begin to count the times I've heard things like "You don't look like a geek" or "You probably play video games to get guys to like you" or "They hired you because of your boobs." I constantly have to prove myself, and it still happens. Between that and the online harassment, it's rough out there.

What tools do you consider crucial to your job?

Wikipedia, IMDb, and the ability to fall asleep in hotels. In terms of the first two, it's all about research. Before an interview, I see the film (if that's what it's for), read everything I can find about it, research every project an actor has done in the past and what they've got coming in the future, read every recent interview they've done, and more. For the second . . . let's just say it's not a good idea to fall asleep during a set visit. I've seen it happen after seventeen-hour flights, in the middle of interviews.

What keeps you going?

I'm inspired by any woman who goes into a career that is considered a "guy thing;" by the writers I have working for me at *Legion of Leia*, whose drive and desire to succeed impress me every day; and by the other women who've spoken out about harassment at work, which happens far more than you might expect.

Any words of advice for would-be bloggers?

Be prepared for this to become your life. It will. There is no way around it. When you're not working, you're going to have to hustle to get your next job. It's all-consuming. Your friends aren't going to understand why you can't make plans or why you keep canceling them. It's worth it. The other thing is, write all the time. If you're trying to break in, you're going to have to give writing samples. Many editors won't care if they're from a site you got paid for. Just show them you can write and they'll probably give you a chance. Write like crazy. Write quickly. Story turnover can be really fast, and you should be able to write up a three-hundred-word news story in less than fifteen minutes. I know it sounds crazy, but it actually becomes a habit.

Oh, and get used to very little sleep.

USE SOCIAL MEDIA

Yes, even if you don't like social media, you're going to have to buckle down and get yourself some online accounts. Without a social media presence, it'll be harder for new people to discover you, old readers to stay connected, and for you to prove your worth to potential future employers and investors. The people who dole out book deals *love* it when their authors come with built-in advertising platforms.

ADVERTISE

Whether it's free advertising through social media/guest spots/bugging your friends or paid ads on other websites, get the word out there. When you're starting out, you should probably try not to spend money on ads since you may not stick with the blog and probably won't have much income. Once you've been at it a while and are sure blogging is something you're really, truly passionate about, don't be afraid to shell out a few gold pieces on advertising networks.

DON'T JUST WORK FOR EXPOSURE BUCKS

There are comfortable, paid writing gigs out there, and they are few and far between. In the distance betwixt such paid gigs, you'll get all kinds of terrible writing offers that want to profit from you in exchange for "exposure."

Actor/blogger/tabletop game video player Wil Wheaton wrote[11] about receiving an inquiry from the Huffington Post, a sprawling online citadel of content. In this inquiry, the Huffington Post requested to repost one of his articles in exchange for increasing his exposure through their huge platform, stating they weren't able to pay their writers at the time.

Frankly, that's bullshit, and Wheaton called them on it. HuffPo was a massive brand earning millions; refusing to pay its writers was a cost-cutting measure that screws over the creatives who make the site what it is. Exposure bucks don't keep the lights on.

There are times when it's absolutely fine to write for free, of course. If, for example, a website is up-front about wanting writers but not being able to afford to pay them yet, like maybe your friend has started a new blog and needs help from others to fill in the gaps, that's fine. And sometimes maybe you feel like writing something without worrying about being paid for it. When writing for free, ask yourself whether the site is a platform capable of promoting you in a way that couldn't be done elsewhere, whether the site's message is something you're comfortable with and want your name associated with, how long you're expected to remain there, and whether having articles on the site will help you get paying jobs down the line.

Ultimately, if you are established, if they ask you to work for them *before* revealing the work would be free, and if it's a company with some income asking to profit from your work, do what you need to get *paid*.

THE BIG QUESTION: HOW THE HELL *DO* I GET PAID TO DO THIS?

The frigid, turgid fact is this—you're not going to make much money at first. It could take years of serious dedication, in fact, before you start to see any kind of appreciable income. Since blogs generally provide their content free of charge and lack any sort of direct product to sell, monetization can be difficult. Building in room for ad banners and the like helps, and programs like Google AdSense™ can give you some nice profits if you're willing to put the time into figuring out search engine optimization (SEO) and its many nuances.

For many pro/semi-pro bloggers, the first paychecks they earn for blogging aren't for things they write for their personal sites; they're for work they do for someone else. Running your own unpaid blog for a few years will build up your audience and résumé so you'll have more clout when applying for paid writing gigs on other sites.

You can also do sponsored articles, where companies pay you to mention or review their service. These gigs generally pay well, *but* to do them well requires serious effort on your part. Readers don't like to feel as if they're being bombarded with ads, and they really don't like feeling that what they're reading has had its integrity compromised. Be selective with your choices of sponsored articles, only incorporating brands and services you personally approve of and feel are appropriate for the audience you've built, and be clear about the compensation you're receiving. If a movie studio pays you to do a preview of their movie, add in a line to your article making that clear. If a company sends you free products to review, let it be known that you received the products for free while still doing your best to review them fairly despite their delicious free-ness.

If you have a post go viral or do a big cross-promotion with a well-known brand, that's a good time to reach out to paying platforms and advertisers to try to rope them into sending some money your way.

Services like Patreon® or Gumroad®, which allow followers to make recurring monetary pledges to you as a creator, make it easier to monetize once you've got something of a following. Patreon and its ilk tend to operate on a reward-tier system; if you want to get people to pledge the higher dollar values for the higher-level rewards, you've got to offer them interesting content to make it worth their cash. Subscription crowdfunding has made it possible for many creators to make nerdy livings. It's not a format that lends itself especially well to bloggers, unfortunately, due to the fact that most bloggers don't tend to generate additional bonus content that people are interested in.

With that in mind, there are a few things you can offer:

- If your blog is oriented around some sort of product, like reviews of knock-off action figures or old movies on DVD/Blu-ray, those can work nicely as membership content (especially if you sign 'em).

- If your blog is *your* blog and not a site run by multiple people, offering links to a special Tumblr full of behind-the-scenes musings, more personal thoughts, and photos can work (though, again, you have to be more careful about the creepo-stalker-obsessive types).

- Online hangouts, video chats, and thank-you credits are standard, straightforward membership content.

- Bloopers are great bonus content, though they're more befitting video content than blogs.

- Autographs are the staple of all famous people. Autograph stuff and sell it.

- If you build things for your blog, like foam weapons and armor or pop culture pewter statues, that stuff makes for *great* membership content, and offering custom content makes for even better expensive, high-tier content.

If the crowdfunding site you're using offers the ability to create multiple tiers of goals ("If my subscribers generate $500 a month, I'll write another two articles a week! If it gets to $1,000 a month, I'll write three more a week!"), then create multiple goal tiers to keep people subscribing, the income increasing, and yourself motivated to do more.

Create clear reward tiers and goals; people aren't as likely to subscribe for additional money if they don't understand what they're subscribing to, or what they're going to get out of the deal.

Ultimately, readers will sometimes buy and subscribe because they like what you're offering, and sometimes they'll do it because they like *you*.

GET A TRUSTED BUSINESS PARTNER

If you have the option to rely on someone with some serious business acumen, you should probably do it. Being creative and being business-minded don't often go hand in hand; for many creatives, the business dealings are easily the most hated part of their jobs. A business partner can act as a gym partner, keeping you accountable for working hard while also taking care of the nitty-gritty technical and money stuff you may not be interested in. That said, this idea supposes that you know someone who is trustworthy, reliable, and business-y who is *also* willing to work for free until the profits start rolling in. In the likely event you don't have someone you can trust and rely on, buckle down and learn to do that stuff yourself.

WORDS FROM WORKING NERDS

Katrina Hill, blogger, actor, producer, Action Flick Chick, author of
Action Movie Freak and *100 Greatest Graphic Novels**

In 2008, my husband and our friends started a website, RocketLlama.com. I happened to watch *Rambo* (the fourth one) for the first time right around then, and it was so amazing that I wanted to tell everyone about it. Inspired by my friends' putting their creative work out there on the web, I wrote a review of *Rambo* for RocketLlama.com. From there the passion grew; I continued to write reviews for their website until one day I decided to create my own website dedicated to action movie news and reviews—ActionFlickChick.com. And from *there* things continued growing, and I got to do all kinds of cool hosting gigs, TV appearances, interviews, book writing, movie reviews, etc.

What tool could you not do without in your job?

I absolutely could not do my job without the Internet and a computer. A lot of writing is researching backstory and trying to gather all kinds of information on the topic you are writing about, and the Internet makes that a lot easier.

Are there any particular obstacles you feel you've had to overcome to get where you are?

---

* Author's note: Katrina also happens to be my super-cool wife.

Sometimes you don't feel like working. You want to sit back and have good things come to you magically, but that isn't how things work. I've had to kick myself a few times to keep writing and keep working hard. This is especially true once you've been working at something for a little while and the excitement and newness begin to wear off or when you have some jobs/opportunities fall through. You have to have the determination and drive to get past that point in order to become successful and stay successful.

Who or what are your inspirations?

My good friends/family who started a little website way back when: Alex,* Nick, and Travis. They definitely served as an inspiration to help me get started in this line of work and continue to do it. It really helps to surround yourself with supportive and creative people.

What tips might you recommend to newcomers looking to get into the business?

Don't be lazy. Work hard. Take whatever job you can get at first, even if it's small, doesn't pay well, or isn't about a topic you absolutely love—do the research and knock it out of the park. This helps build up your résumé, credentials, and reputation.

Meet your freaking deadlines! Not much is more frustrating than working with someone who can't turn in assignments on time.

Don't be a douche nugget online or offline. If you are a joy to work with, then people will continue to work with you and recommend you to others. If you are a douche nugget, no one will want to work with you again.

---

* Author's note: Hey, that's me!

KEEP ON TRUCKIN' AND KEEP ON POSTIN'

Even the most fun career in the world isn't fun every single day. You may be tired of posting videos or writing blog posts, but you've *got* to stick with it. The number-one reason could-be-professional nerds fail is because they get tired of what they're doing or get distracted with other projects/real life and then lose what audience they've managed to accumulate. The Internet is a vast cosmic space filled with the charnel husks of dead blogs and video channels; keep posting, space cowboy, lest your site wither away into nothingness.

BEWARE SHIFTY WRITING GIGS

I once had an offer of a writing gig with a video game website with a rather misleading set-up for paying its writers. Essentially, I had to write twentyish articles a month for them, for free, with their editor getting final say on both what I was writing and how I was writing it, and then after that I would get paid for any approved articles. That's a *whole* lotta work they were asking me to do for free, and even *if* they approved subsequent articles beyond my free ones (which seemed unlikely), the pay-per-article rate was almost nothing when averaged in with the freebies. The editor kept emphasizing how his writers got paid often and well and had the freedom to write whatever they wanted . . . with approval. As you might have guessed, I passed. I understand the difficulty of getting enough money to pay writers what they deserve; however, as I said before, people need to get paid for their work if there's any money to be had. If that site even remotely had the writer's best interest at heart, why not pay them for each article, even at a low pay rate, rather than requiring so many free articles per month?

A friend had written a few free articles for a website before requesting to link to one of these free articles on a paying website that she was also writing for. Her editor flipped out, calling her greedy for having the ovaries to try to profit from what she'd written.

Another friend wrote for a site that paid low, but well enough that it was worth the work. When payday arrived, however, the site owners made excuses about delaying payment and continued this pattern for months until the friend got sick of writing for them and left. Later, the friend found out that this site was notorious for doing this to all of their employees; they'd rope in accomplished writers, then wring a few months' worth of free articles out of them with the promise of pay without ever actually intending to pay them. If someone is supposed to pay you, do *not* let them slide on being late. Call them out on it, and if they get mad when you bring it up, it's time for you to hop on your horse and ride off into the sunset.

These stories are hardly unique, and the moral is always the same—you've got to look out for yourself and not let your drive to succeed overwhelm your spidey-sense for getting screwed over. The people who are most commonly the victims of scams are those who are too desperate for money to take a moment to think about what's happening.

DON'T GET SCAMMED IN OTHER WAYS

Other common scams and sleazy situations to look out for in the blogging world include:

- **Content farms**, which are websites that pay hordes of freelance writers next to nothing to create articles that are essentially piles of links and buzzwords designed to get the site owners advertising money and better placement in search engines

- **Guest-post scams**, wherein the "guest poster" writes a post for your site that is actually a paid advertisement they can pocket the money while you get nothing

- **Commenter bots**, who will litter your site with comments linking to shady sites and spyware (most hosting platforms have built-in ways of detecting and deterring these pests)

- **Offers to revamp your site** from "experts" who really want you to pay them to suggest that you change your website's theme

- **Offers to increase your traffic/follower count** (generally through the use of bots, which can get you banned lickety-split)

- **Notifications that your blog has won an award** you've never heard of (generally a way for the award-giver to get free advertising on your site)

- **Offers to enter a blogging contest** (generally a money pyramid where you have very little chance of winning or earning money and a very high chance that the people organizing it will net a ton of cash)

With blogging, as in real life, go with your gut and stay away from shady-feeling deals. If something seems too good to be true or like you're the one getting one up on the other person and they don't realize it, you're probably 'bout to get scammed.

DON'T GET TOO PUBLIC

Generally speaking, it's great to have an open, trusting personality. On the Internet, though, that can be a dangerous thing as you'll find there's no shortage of crazy assholes there. Don't be too forthcoming with personal information, especially if you're a member of a minority population, as you're more likely to become targeted by one of the aforementioned crazy assholes. If you're utilizing social media heavily, scrub your personal info and open a separate account specifically for friends and family, perhaps one with a pseudonym and a profile image of something other than yourself. Don't fill out unnecessary information on social media, make your passwords tougher than PetNameAndMyDateOfBirthOrYearIGraduated or any variation of 1234567890 (which are a couple of the most commonly used passwords, so if those are your passwords *change them right the hell now)*, answer password security questions with weird answers only you will know, use multi-factor authentication when you can, etc. This will help keep down the number of potential stalkers and hackers to a minimum.

DON'T OBSESS OVER NUMBERS

You'll drive yourself crazy checking to see how many hits you have every single day. Keep an eye on the numbers, checking them periodically without the expectation of seeing much action early on. Don't let random, wild downswings get you too down (while taking full advantage of any big upswings).

BRANCH OUT

The last piece of advice about running a blog might be the most important: It doesn't have to be the only thing you do! There are so, so many delicious kinds of geekery out there. Explore them! If you're looking for something that pairs nicely with article-writing this time of year, might I suggest the fine, heady aroma of videography?

CHAPTER TWO

VIDEO

Influencers, content creators, YouTube superstars . . . though no one can agree on an exact job title, most can agree that the advent of online videos has created a new type of career path, one that puts the power in the hands of creators.*

What is it about online videos that draws people to the format? For some, it's the interactivity of making videos—of connecting with people from across the globe despite never physically meeting them. For others, it's the ability of online videos' to enable film-making types like actors and directors to take control of their careers and make the sort of roles and stories *they* want to make without waiting for cigar-chomping guys in suits to give them the go-ahead. For others still, it's simply a means of expression. Sometimes that expression is "Let me show you how to put on makeup!" or "Sweet pants-melting *Satan,* these old video games are hard!" or "GYARGH!! I hate every single last one of you!"

Regardless of *why* you decide to tube, this career has become among the most desired, most sought-after jobs out there, mixing the thrill of celebrity with the comfort of working from your own home. The history of Internet videos is short and sweet, and while the Internet landscape today is very different than it was in the '90s and '00s†, there are still plenty of lessons modern video creators can learn from their Internet ancestors.

---

* Note that for this section, like the rest of the book, I'm not going to cover the more adult-themed ways a person can make a living through online videos. There are many reasons why they won't be covered in the book, not the least of which is that making adult videos generally isn't very nerdy.
† Pronounced "nineties" and "ooh-oohs."

THE HISTORY OF INTERNET VIDEO CONTENT CREATORS

I'm not talking about the goobers and goofballs behind early Internet phenomena like "Numa Numa" or "Star Wars Kid," I'm talking about the folks who deliberately poured their heart-blood into making moving pictures for complete strangers and received a glittering gold reward for their efforts: the early pioneers of online short films, web series, and animated series who were bold enough to trailblaze a career from something that hadn't existed a decade earlier.

Avid gamer Felicia Day was hopelessly addicted to the titanic crack pipe known as *World of Warcraft*. Sick of the mercenary nature of most acting roles, Day tried to take control of her life and *WoW* addiction by writing *The Guild,* a sitcom pilot* about a group of MMO (Massively Multiplayer Online game) guildmates trying to balance the demands of their real and virtual lives. Hollywood being Hollywood, the suits in charge didn't understand the appeal of such a show and declined, so Day instead turned to the online world. Through a combination of smart writing, powerful comedic chops, good timing, and generous fans, Day and her team of writers and co-stars triumphed, building what is still one of the most popular web series of all time.

Day's success with *The Guild* inspired *Buffy the Vampire Slayer* creator Joss Whedon to make his own web series, *Dr. Horrible's Sing-Along Blog*, casting Day and her fellow Whedonverse vet Nathan Fillion alongside Neil Patrick Harris to create a dramedy/musical too eclectic for the traditional Hollywood system. *Dr. Horrible* became a powerful cult classic, selling countless DVDs, stacks of merch, and getting aired on the CW Network in what Day described as a "big victory as far as mainstream Hollywood acknowledgment of web series as a legitimate format [goes]."[12]

Day continued refining her craft as a writer and performer to later star in the Kickstarter-funded *Mystery Science Theater 3000* revival and her own successful YouTube channel, Geek and Sundry. Like many YouTube channels,

---

* A *pilot* is an industry term for a singular episode of an episodic series designed to sell it to a network. Hey! I see you, rolling your eyes, thinking, *Yeah, I already knew that*. There are people who didn't and probably appreciate not having to try to figure out what flying a plane has to do with making an episodic series.

Geek and Sundry focuses on a particular theme while also focusing on a specific team of on-camera personalities. When people watch Wil Wheaton's *TableTop*, they don't do it just to see wild and esoteric board games get played, they do it because of Wheaton and his cohorts' affable enthusiasm. Viewers don't just tune in to *Critical Role* to hear Matthew Mercer's dulcet tones as he DMs sessions of Dungeons & Dragons; he and his party are professional performers and players who know how to create one hell of an entertaining story.

On the animated side of things, we have hits such as: *Homestar Runner*, a comedy series that gained popularity primarily through word of mouth; *Red vs. Blue*, a Halo parody series that became so popular, its creators got the chance to be in the game series that inspired them (and create a media juggernaut with the anime series *RWBY*); *Dragon Ball Z Abridged*, a comedy series that lovingly recreates *Dragon Ball Z* in a parody style reminiscent of Adult Swim's early works; and *Homestuck*, a multimedia hit that requires a long-ass wiki to fully understand.

Not all early web series were of the grassroots variety. *The Spot*, described as "*Melrose Place*–on-the-web"[13] back when both *Melrose Place* and referring to the Internet as "the web" were remotely in style, was a more corporate affair than the other early web series. *The Spot* mixed blog entries, e-mail, static images, and video to create a highly interactive story that fans could influence. Its writers often changed the directions of its melodramatic gosh-it's-hard-being-young-and-beautiful storylines based on the fickle fans, giving Hollywood its first taste of the potential power of online video content. While *The Spot* flourished briefly, it eventually became less of a spot and more of a muddy blotch due to corporate greed from the higher-ups, resulting in serious behind-the-scenes drama. Sadly, it was cancelled after a few short years.

Today's online video landscape is as much about the person in the videos as it is their actual content. Before you can reach the success of Felicia Day and the like, you'll need to put in some serious prep, starting with figuring out what kind of content you're trying to be successful with.

CHOOSE YOUR DESTINY: TYPES OF ONLINE CHANNELS

Channel contents can range from the gentle blandness of videos of shoes being shined to the haunting weirdness of someone making mannequins sing about how fantastic they feel in rooms with taped-up garbage bags over the windows. Most channels, however, fall into a few basic categories.*

GENERIC/"PERSONALITY"
Example channels: Felix "PewDiePie" Kjellberg, Mark "Markiplier" Fischbach, Jenna "JennaMarbles" Mourey, The Fine Bros, Ryan "NigaHiga" Higa

PewDiePie and company are among the most powerful video stars on the Internet. The content of their channels tends to be somewhat eclectic, with everything from makeup tutorials to comedy sketches to gaming videos to kids reacting to kids reacting to kids.

These folks have, by and large, achieved their fame through perseverance, good luck, and force of personality. Channels like these are probably the hardest to make grow, yet are invariably the most pursued style of channel. Countless would-be YouTubers upload videos of their thoughts and reactions online, counting on their raw personalities to entertain the audience. While these channels *can* be done well, they're a dime-a-dozen-to-the-thirteenth-power. The examples I gave at the start of this section are the exceptions to the rule that, if you want to have a successful video channel, you should focus on a subject other than yourself.†

- ◆ **PROS**: Largely require the efforts of only one person—*you*; they're cheap to make; you get all the credit

- ◆ **CONS**: Hard to grow; content doesn't generate organically; low-effort videos are especially bland and boring; this content can really suck if you don't have a good editor; you take all the blame when things aren't good; personal attacks from trolls get exceptionally personal

---

* Keep in mind that this list is in no way exhaustive and focuses mostly on geeky, English-language YouTubers because I'm sadly monolingual and can't vet the content of non-English YouTubers very well. Also know any and all of these channels could disappear at any time due to the creators quitting/YouTube getting bought out/zombie apocalypse.
† That's not a judgment on you, dear reader. I'm sure you're a lovely and interesting person.

SKETCH COMEDY

Example channels: Mega64, Derrick Comedy, ERB (Epic Rap Battles of History), Smosh, Rhett & Link, Lonely Island

Before Mega64 was a multimedia empire, it was a group of goofs making parody videos of *Resident Evil 4* and *Assassin's Creed*. Before Donald Glover stepped into the smooth mustache of Lando Calrissian, he and his comedy pals were performing sketches about trying to resist the erotic enticements of a bowl of fruit. Sketch comedy is a noble art form dating back to the vaudeville era, a time when people wore top hats and fluffy dresses and big mustaches and *talked like this, friend!** At its most artistic, this performance style can provide razor-sharp insight into the state of society; at its goofiest, it's a bunch of funny people trying to make one another (and hopefully others) laugh.

While sketch comedy started on stage, eventually it broke away from its show-timey roots to find a wider audience through television and, ultimately, the Internet. Online videos turned out to be a great format for sketches, as Internet audiences are often searching for a quick laugh they can share with their friends without worrying about things like continuity. Even popular television shows like *Key & Peele* and *SNL* have gotten big hits when posting their sketches and digital shorts on YouTube.

- **PROS**: Can combine challenging social commentary with comedy; really fun to make with friends; one smash-hit video can lead to a big break more easily than it would with another type of channel

- **CONS**: Require more prep-time, thought, and collaborative effort than many other types of channels

GAMING AND LET'S PLAY

Example channels: Game Grumps, Maximilian Dood, Geek & Sundry (*TableTop*, *Critical Role*), VanossGaming, JackSepticEye

---

* Note: For best effect, please read italicized portion in a vaudevillian voice.

Gaming channels provide roughly two types of content: walkthroughs and "Let's Play" videos. Walkthroughs focus on the minutiae of games, helping struggling players find buried secrets or tips on how to beat that one dick boss who keeps killing them. These are good for video creators who have the knowledge and skill but perhaps aren't as goofy or lively as other performers.* Generally, getting the biggest hits on walkthroughs will require you to quickly play through popular games so you can get your footage online and stake your claim as *the* definitive video guide to getting Mario's hat down from the tree in the desert world.

Let's Play videos stem from the comedy forums at Something Awful,[14] where folks play through games and post videos and screenshots of their experience with their commentary and, often, with input from their eager audience. Some of these Let's Plays are informative, others humorous, and others still focus on breaking open their game of choice to explore its inner workings.

The question you may be asking is: Why would anyone spend their time watching others play through games? Because Let's Plays provide a way for gamers to connect with other gamers, past and present; to relive the thrills and spills of their favorite games; and to feel a sense of community (and, in the case of streaming Let's Plays, immediacy) not found in playing games alone. Humans are social creatures that crave connection on a deep, fundamental level. Gaming can be a lonely hobby, often enjoyed alone; while some time alone is fine, too much is bad for you, leading to disruptions in our perceptions, behaviors, and bodies.[15] For some, Let's Plays provide a way of undoing some of that isolation, and for others it's simply a way to share the joy of their favorite hobby.

- ◆ **PROS**: Content ideas are easy to generate; good for generating multiple revenue sources through streaming; gamers are ravenous for new content

- ◆ **CONS**: Content will be most successful if you're a highly skilled gamer and/or have an energetic personality; gamers can be seriously entitled jerks; not a viable choice if you don't like video games (unless you're Conan O'Brien)

---

* If you are a bit on the serious side, you might want to consider finding yourself a goofy cohost who can play off of your stoicism. It worked for *Mythbusters*.

HOW-TO AND TUTORIALS

Example channels: Bright Side, Rosana Pansino/Nerdy Nummies, Binging with Babish, Christen Dominique, Laura Lee

How-to channels focus on instructing viewers looking to broaden their skillsets. They tend to be laser focused and get to the point quickly, without a lot of different types of videos on their channel. If someone needs to know how to build a garage and they come to your home-building channel, the last thing they're going to want to sift through are comedy sketches featuring your uncle and his unfunny friends pantsing one another at a bat mitzvah.

How-to channels are a great choice for people with a very particular set of skills; if there's something you know well, something you stay up-to-date on and are always striving to get better at, it might not be a bad idea to share that knowledge with the world.

- **PROS:** Easier to gain followers due to high skill requirement; videos tend to continue gaining views over long periods of time; content is incredibly helpful to those who need specific tutorials; easier to monetize due to built-in presence of potential brands through material and tools

- **CONS:** Higher cost of entry; higher skill requirement; higher tools and materials requirement

CRAFTING

Example channels: Awe Me/Man at Arms, Simone Giertz, How to Cake it with Yolanda Gampp, Skallagrim, Alec Steele

Though they share some surface similarities, the biggest difference between a crafting channel and a how-to channel is that a how-to channel is about teaching you how to do something specific while a crafting channel is more about inspiring, educating, and entertaining people by making things they probably won't make themselves. Yolanda Gampp's Giant Chocolate Éclair or Giant Red Velvet Steak Cake aren't practical treats to make for your family, they're entertaining ways of getting people to think creatively about cooking. Simone Giertz doesn't make alarm bots that slap her awake and tangle her hair in the mechanism in the hopes that viewers will copy her to get their hair ripped out first thing in the morning, she does it to entertain and draw in potential newcomers to the fields of engineering and robotics. Man at Arms certainly doesn't seem to be recommending that you recreate Cloud Strife's Buster Sword in your own home, but watching the trouble they go through to forge it (and how awesome it looks when chopping things up) may give you the idea to become a blacksmith or metallurgist yourself.

- ◆ **PROS**: Easy to gain followers due to high skill requirement; little competition; easier to monetize due to creation of physical products that can be sold
- ◆ **CONS**: Requires large investiture of resources for each video; greater research requirements than other channels

LIFE HACKS

Example channels: Expert Village/eHow, Howcast, I Like to Make Stuff, HawkGuruHacker, Morena DIY, Mr. Gear, The Q

Life Hacks are a strange intersection of crafting and how-to. It's a term that previously meant "little known but valuable tip" but has now become so overused that it just means "a thing you can do." Life Hacks can provide useful, esoteric ways of doing things better. Sometimes, however, they're highly impractical, offering solutions that are worse than the problem they're trying to solve (such as using toothpaste and soda to wash things when soap will do a better job and won't leave your stuff sticky). Life Hacks are frequently the YouTube equivalent of old late-night infomercials, offering impractical solutions to problems no one has. That said, even the most impractical Life Hacks are good exercises in divergent thinking.

- ◆ **PROS**: Quick and easy to put together
- ◆ **CONS**: Hard to create new and useful Life Hack ideas

UNBOXING VIDEOS AND PRODUCT REVIEWS

Example channels: Unbox Therapy, Grav3yard Girl, Ryan ToysReview, LeoKim Video

What's in the box? *What's in the box???* We, like Brad Pitt in *Se7en*, are endlessly curious to know what's in the box, and unboxing videos are the answer. While Brad Pitt and Gwyneth Paltrow weren't so lucky when it came to the contents of *their* box, viewers are when it comes to unboxing videos. This channel type often features gentle voice-overs while opening up, unwrapping, and showing off the features of different kinds of toys. Some are toys for kids, some are electronic toys for grown-ups, but the intent is the same—unboxing videos let viewers feel like *they're* getting to play with fancy new stuff, and, in the case of videos marketed to kids, it will make the viewer themselves feel like they're being played with.

- ◆ **PROS**: Early content ideas are easy to generate; easy advertising-integration opportunities; easy to get freebies

- ◆ **CONS**: Strict requirements regarding ethical advertising; content ideas may run low if you choose a line of products that has a limited number of variants; new channels won't get freebies from the companies they're reviewing, so recurring costs can add up

ASMR/RELAXATION CHANNELS

Example channels: ASMRrequests, Heather Feather, Massage ASMR, GentleWhispering, GibiASMR

The autonomous sensory meridian response (ASMR) is a nonscientific term for a phenomenon that, despite its apparent online prevalence, is relatively unstudied. ASMR refers to a tingly, pleasing sensation moving up the spine and back of the head, often described as feeling like having your brain purr. Whether ASMR is a distinct phenomenon or something else people are confusedly mislabeling as ASMR is a matter for debate; meanwhile, the videos designed to cause ASMR are very real and very profitable.

Every night, countless insomniacs flock to YouTube looking for videos to help them punch the Sandman in his stupid face so they can get a few hours' sleep. Such videos have a range of content to them. Some are obviously relaxing, like narrators gently explaining massage techniques as they massage someone or soothing music set over a nature scene. Some are oddly intimate, with "ASMRtists" giving first-person cranial nerve examinations, haircuts, and makeup tutorials to the camera. Some are a bit unusual, like videos of people pretending to be soft-spoken plague doctors, holodeck operators, and characters from pop culture.

- ◆ **PROS**: Very low cost to start; only requires a single person to set up and execute; viewers are generally friendly if you're male

- ◆ **CONS**: Making high-quality videos requires expensive microphones; can be exhausting to do alone; can feel extremely silly and/or awkward to pretend to massage a camera or give it a haircut; hard to do if you don't have a soothing voice; viewers are generally creepy if you're female

MUSIC
Example channels: Smooth McGroove, Taylor Davis, OC Remix, Dwelling of Duels, Neil Cicierega*

Since the advent of the music industry, we've had gatekeepers at the very top dictating what sort of music others could listen to. If your sound was too weird, too experimental, or went against the grain too hard, the likelihood of eager ears ever getting to listen to it was low. Today, anyone can get their music out there, no matter how nontraditional their channel may be. Smooth McGroove performs a capella renditions of famous video game tunes, while Taylor Davis creates violin-oriented remixes of film, TV, and video game scores. Neil Cicierega has several albums of eclectic mash-ups of pop music

---

* There are a number of celebrity musicians who got their start on YouTube and the like. We're not talking about those goobers, we're talking about the more normal/nerdy folks who happen to make their living posting music videos.

(and what seems to be an unhealthy obsession with Smash Mouth's "All Star"). These folks have had stirring success through their online videos, allowing them to find fans who would have never been given the chance to hear their music in years past.

- **PROS**: Can be monetized both through videos and through sale of audio; music fans are generally pretty chill peeps
- **CONS**: Very high skill requirement; good-looking music videos require serious work to shoot; lots of restrictions and royalty issues if you primarily post covers of other people's songs

SHORT FILM

Example channels: RocketJump, Corridor Digital, Film Riot, Final Cut King

Thanks to the increasing power of computers (and their increased availability), it's easier than ever for aspiring filmmakers to create the short video story brewing in their hearts. Short-film channels are often special effects-oriented, as it's easier to grab attention online if you've got something flashy to do the grabbing with. Plus the format is flexible enough to make it easier to integrate products once you start getting offers for advertising money.

- **PROS**: Less competition due to comparatively high cost of entry; trendy short films have an easier time generating views and going viral
- **CONS**: Making good short films is friggin' hard, people

ANALYSIS

Example channels: Feminist Frequency, Every Frame a Painting, Pop Culture Detective, Lindsay Ellis/Nostalgia Chick, The Film Theorists/The Game Theorists

Analysis channels turn a critical eye toward their topic of choice, discussing the good and the bad, the smart and the dumb, the well known and the esoteric. These channels teach us audience members how to think critically and absorb media critically. Tony Zhou's Every Frame a Painting, for example, generally focuses on particular film directors or cinematographic techniques to educate future filmmakers and storytellers. Anita Sarkeesian's Feminist Frequency looks at pop culture (primarily video games) to discuss the ways in which different stories represent women.*

- ♦ **PROS**: Fosters conversation and encourages repeat viewers who are often contemplative and conversational
- ♦ **CONS**: Analysis channels are troll magnets that will very likely draw the jerks away from their bridges and three billy goats gruff

EDUCATION
Example channels: CrashCourse, VSauce, ASAPScience, minutephysics, TEDTalks

The ability to concisely convey complex subjects in an entertaining way is one of the most important skills a human being can have; the spread of information is what elevates us above the rest of the critters we call roommates on this big ol' planet. If you're someone with a strong background in research—hopefully with extensive experience in a particular field of study—and you have a knack for boiling big concepts down to their diluted essence for easy swallowing, an educational YouTube channel might be just the ticket for you.

---

* While analysis channels foster discussion easily, they also tend to draw greater criticism and flat-out hatred, particularly if you're a member of a marginalized population. Trolls seem to follow Anita Sarkeesian's every move, all because she had the audacity to 1. be a woman, and 2. talk about how poorly represented women are in video games. Sarkeesian's frequent collaborator, Jonathan McIntosh, discusses many of the same themes as Sarkeesian on his Pop Culture Detective channel, and yet he gets only a fraction of the criticism she gets and far fewer threats of death/rape/doxxing.

- **PROS**: Gains numerous views over long periods of time; helps increase the world's general knowledge levels; helps students who are confused and desperate because they have a paper on *Noh* theater due in three hours and they don't know what the hell *Noh* theater is

- **CONS**: Requires a strong knowledge base; videos require a high degree of research; viewers can be argumentative beyond what's reasonable or productive

PRANKS/SOCIAL EXPERIMENTS

Example channels: No one worth mentioning

While pranks and "social experiments" make for a somewhat popular style of YouTube channel, they also present a major problem—the people making those channels are being serious jerks and exploiting others for money. Pranking your friends and family gets old *fast* and will lead to their resenting you for feeling like they can never fully be at ease if you're around.

Pranking strangers is even worse, because these strangers 1) didn't ask to be involved with your dumb video, 2) get nothing out of being involved, and 3) are generally made out to look really foolish.

"Social experiments" are the bottom of the barrel because they're frequently fake while having deep-rooted elements of sexism, racism, and bigotry to them, as exemplified by the number of "social experiments" that involve sexually harassing women or doing things in the "hood." From a scientific perspective, these "experiments" are anything but; they lack control groups, independent/dependent variables, ethical codes of conduct, and all the other stuff that makes science *science*. If you want to make a prank or "social experiment" channel, be better than that—the world has enough jerks in it already.

OUTSIDER ART

Example channels: Poppy, HowToBasic, LasagnaCat, Hydraulic Press Channel

Here we have the truly avant-garde, the beautiful post-modern weirdos who turn the mirror back on YouTube by eschewing tradition. What they do is bizarre and fantastic, and they do it not because they crave the likes and subscribers but because it must be done. Poppy, a parody of YouTube Personalities, posts apology videos apologizing for controversies that don't exist, repeats the mantra "I love my fans" for forty seconds straight, and argues with a mannequin wearing a birdcage. HowToBasic describes itself as a handy how-to channel, yet its videos are from the perspective of a deranged nude man destroying roasted turkeys and smashing eggs. LasagnaCat is a *Garfield* parody series that goes so far beyond simple parody that I simply don't have room to get into it all. Hydraulic Press Channel posts videos of stuff getting smooshed by a hydraulic press. If you're tired of the Reaction Videos and generic Let's Play channels, examine the avant-garde and consider joining their beautifully weird ranks.

- ◆ **PROS**: Highly unique content
- ◆ **CONS**: You may go insane

WORDS FROM WORKING NERDS

Allen Pan, YouTuber and science communicator

I've always had a sort of bucket list of projects—things I wanted to make because I thought the idea was cool but that I didn't have an immediate reason to actually build. In 2015, I realized I'd never get around to building those cool ideas unless I had an excuse to, so I created a YouTube channel called Sufficiently Advanced as a reference to the Arthur C. Clarke quote. I figured having a YouTube channel would finally be the excuse I needed to start building. The idea was that I'd build functional, real-life versions of sci-fi and fantasy gadgets and weapons using contemporary, off-the-shelf technology (hence the Clarke quote). I thought that if I kept at it, it might pay for itself in about a year. In October [2015], I uploaded a video of a replica of Mjolnir (Thor's Hammer) I'd made, and in the first week, that video got over seven million views. It was the second video I had ever uploaded to YouTube! Suddenly it seemed like I could do this sort of thing for a living, rather than just a side hobby. I've been doing that ever since!

What sort of work goes into each project?

When I start a project, there's a ton of research up-front. Not only for the build and what technology I can use to replicate some science-magic object, but also the fictional canon of that object. Building a real version of a fictional gadget almost always comes down to interpretation, since fictional gadgets are rarely constrained by real-world physics. Once I have a few ideas, I start testing for feasibility. A lot of the stuff I build doesn't have much precedent, so there's usually a lot of experimenting to be done to make sure the idea physically works. Once I'm confident that everything will probably work okay, I start the final build and refine as I go. This is when I start thinking about what the final video is going to look like and start planning out the shots I want in my head. When the build is done, I start filming the results, and I sometimes have to backfill by recreating parts of the build process on camera. It might not be efficient, but I can't stand being constrained by a camera when building. I'd rather recreate a necessary shot of me building a part than worry about lighting and angles while I'm actually trying to build that part. Once I've got most of the footage I need, I start editing and usually end up cutting out about half of the stuff I've planned and scripted. You have to keep videos tight on YouTube, and I tend to overexplain things anyway. Once the video is done and uploaded, I sleep for a couple days and start planning out the next video!

How do you go about explaining what you do to people outside of nerdy/Internet-y careers, like kindly grandparents or easily confused in-laws?

Saying I'm a "YouTuber" usually suffices actually, since a lot of people have a general understanding of what that means. The most common follow-up question is how I make money, at which point I have a canned and concise explanation of how ad revenue works.

What was your first paid, professionally nerdy project?

The first thing I did "professionally" on YouTube was a video series I filmed with Mouser Electronics. I was tasked with building a real flying version of Captain America's shield (a foam shield mounted on a quadcopter) and was to compete head-to-head with their brand ambassador, who was building an Iron Man gauntlet with a real burning laser inside. The brand ambassador turned out to be former Mythbuster Grant Imahara, and the whole experience was ridiculously awesome. Mouser flew me out to their headquarters in Texas, and Grant and I faced off in a balloon-popping competition with our builds. That's when I felt like I had really made it on YouTube.

How important do you feel social media is for your line of work?

It's very important but not necessary. On YouTube, you eat what you kill. People can have successful YouTube channels and careers without ever touching social media, but they would do even better if they did. Audiences really respond to creator interaction, and nowadays there's an expectation that you'll be able to talk to your favorite content creators directly on Twitter or Instagram. If you can provide that interaction, your audience will be more likely to sit through an ad or pitch in a couple bucks on Patreon. So not strictly necessary, but it can help a lot.

What tool or material do you like working with the least?

I hate Photoshop®. Not for any technical reasons; mostly because the video thumbnail is always the last thing I end up working on for a video, and it's almost always at 2:00 A.M. I've just associated opening Photoshop with dread and exhaustion.

Are there any particular obstacles you feel you've had to overcome to get where you are?

It takes money to make money! I was extremely poor when I started my channel, and it can be tough to make good content when you're using cardboard boxes as tripods. It's no coincidence that so many YouTubers are middle-class white dudes; it's a lot easier to have a successful channel if you've already got free time and resources. Fortunately, I basically won the virality lottery and was able to get by while filming on my phone and editing with free software until I saved up for nicer stuff!

Who or what are your inspirations?

Other YouTubers! Specifically William Osman, Peter Sripol, Evan Kale, and James Hobson. We've got a secret chat group online where we discuss YouTube-y things, and their help and support has been invaluable.

What tips might you recommend to newcomers looking to get into the business?

I'd recommend focusing on making good, unique content on a consistent schedule. Don't chase fads, and make your audience feel like they're your friend. A small and loyal audience is better than a large and fair-weather audience. If you can do all that, your odds of succeeding on YouTube are much greater!

BE A NEIGHBOR

Regardless of what sort of channel you want to create, if you intend your viewing audience to be kids—particularly very young kids—then you should be careful about how your content is presented. Kids are impressionable. Incredibly, adorably, *dangerously* impressionable. For years, there's been a seedy underbelly to online video content in the form of bizarre, barely regulated "kids" content that preys on the tendency of children to watch things based on key images or words without any regard for content. Videos with titles like "Spider-Man and Elsa Drink Poison from the Toilet" or "Peppa Pig Pulls the Legs off of Peppa Pig Junior" draw kids in and then often disturb them or reinforce dangerous behavior. Most of these videos seem to be made by shady overseas companies spending pennies to buy cheap animations and abuse SEO (search engine optimization).

Fred Rogers, better known as Mr. Rogers to most of America, believed children are constantly learning and that children's entertainers have a responsibility to present children with content that's respectful, positive, and educational. There are more than enough people in the world willing to exploit kids for a few quick bucks. If you're going to make content for the next generations, be like Mr. Rogers—be a neighbor.

STARTING POINT: ONLINE VIDEOS

Now that you have some idea of the sorts of video channel you might want to start, it's time to make like an ill-advised horror movie character and split up for supplies.

- ◆ **A camera.** Lower-quality video is fine for streaming since many viewers don't have fast enough Internet to stream fully HD video. If you're not streaming, then the more HD you can go, the better. Don't, however, feel like you need to buy some $1,000+ DSLR camera. Plenty of great channels get by on far cheaper equipment; some even use the most versatile and expensive piece of hardware they already own—their phones.

- **A great microphone.** Viewers are more forgiving of a fuzzy video than they are of fuzzy sound. Get a good mic and test that everything is coming through nice and clear. The built-in mics on computers and cameras usually suck the snot from a dead ogre's nose. Read some reviews so you can find a maneuverable, crystal-clear, free-standing mic within your price range.

- **A green screen, if you're feeling fancy.** The big secret about green screens is that they're just big green blankets.

- **Lights.** Having fluctuating light levels is distracting to the eye and mighty unprofessional. Get some lights to keep your beautiful *punim* lit up nice and consistent. Nice, shiny daylight is your best lighting, but that's not always possible. When it's not, a three-light set-up will keep your lighting from making you look like a murderer watching partying teenagers through a slit in the windows. When *that's* not possible, get a lamp or two and test the lighting until you find an arrangement that doesn't make you look so serial killer-esque.

- **Editing software.** If you're only streaming videos, you don't really have to worry about editing anything together. If you want to do something more complex, however, you'll need a program to edit it. Sony® VEGAS®, Adobe® Premiere® with After Effects®, Final Cut Pro®, Avid® (which is powerful but has a steep learning curve), DaVinci Resolve®, and the no-cost Lightworks are all solid choices.

- **Some friends who will work for free/cheap.** If you're running a solo channel—something more vlog-like—then doing it all alone is much more feasible. If you want to create short films or sketch comedy, however, get some dang friends in there to do it with you.

- **Makeup.** The *Planet Earth* documentary series debuted when HD footage was relatively new, and I still remember how disgusting it was to watch a bunch of lions tear into a fly-swarmed wildebeest carcass in full HD. If you go in front of an HD camera with no makeup, poor lighting, and poor set-up, don't be surprised if you end up looking like that dead wildebeest. Even the most beautiful people in the world can look awful if you catch them unprepared—think of all those awful paparazzi shots of celebrities looking washed-out and double-chinned. If you're going to have your face on camera, *especially* if you're doing up-close work for vlogs and the like, you should know a few basic makeup tips: Use moisturizer, add a little contour to help your face pop better on camera, find a makeup shade one shade darker than your skin tone if you're using a three-source light set-up, blend the edges, be careful not to make yourself look washed-out with too much powder, and minimize shiny skin because that'll show up like a freakin' lighthouse on camera.

ANSWERING THE BIG QUESTIONS

In the early days of getting your video channel going, you'll have a few important questions you need to answer. First, decide who you want your audience to be. Are you hoping to entertain children with educational antics? Do you want to do in-depth analyses to appeal to academic adults? Prefer to keep it fast, furious, and full of curses to snag the ever-elusive tween audience? Figuring out a target demographic is point number one on pretty much any marketing plan, so think about who you want watching your content, to better create content that caters to their tastes.

What kind of budget do you have to work with? Even seemingly inexpensive channels oriented around Let's Plays and reaction videos require capture cards for non-Mac computers, high-quality cameras, microphones, etc., so you'll have to work with whatever budget you have.

What's your plan for your channel? Do you hope to still be making videos ten, twenty years down the line, or are you looking for a fun hobby that may or may not lead to long-term success? There's no right or wrong answer here, only the answer that fits you.

If you're having trouble moving beyond basic film set-ups, try enlisting young filmmakers who need the experience. We writers have the benefit of being able to go and write at any moment, should we so choose. An actor who is eager to act, however, can't just sit in their room and act for a few hours.* Directors, editors, sound technicians . . . all those lovely folks who make videos happen need to work with a team, so scour around to see who might work for the sheer experience of *getting* some experience. Be willing to pay them back by working for them when they need it, too; if time is money, you can pay people with your time when you don't have the money.

---

* Well, I suppose they could, but good luck getting anyone to buy tickets

WORDS FROM WORKING NERDS

Lindsay Ellis, who, in her self-titled Youtube channel, uses video essays to garner in-depth discussions of films

How do you explain what you do to others?

The thing I've found about new media is that if [people are] not in the life, they don't really care. I'll try to explain it in the simplest terms, like ad revenue or crowdfunding, and generally they'll be like, "Uhhh, that's nice." If I say I work for PBS or I'm an independent contractor, they understand that, so usually I'll talk about freelancing for other vendors that people have actually heard of. That's an option a lot of YouTubers do, that [others] understand.

Your video analysis of the 2017 Netflix film *Bright* clocks in at nearly forty-five minutes, and your videos often are in the fifteen- to twenty-minute range. How long does it take to create such works?

[*Bright*] was an outlier and should not be counted. That one only took about two weeks because it was fueled by hate and the knowledge that no one was going to care about *Bright* in a week. So for that one I sort of jokingly sent a message to Deron (YouTube's Rap Critic) and I was like, "Hey, you should rap about this orc cop guy," and the next day Deron's like, "I did it." Everything kind of fell together. That one was unusually fast.

Normally it'll be closer to two months. Like, the *Hobbit* videos, start to finish, we started in November—and [they were] three great big projects—and those were released through March and April, so that was closer to five months. On average, I would say for your basic twenty-minute video, one month. For the more research-heavy ones, six to eight weeks. For the really big projects, closer to three or four months.

As someone who often collaborates with other video critics, what do you feel are the advantages of working with others?

On the whole, collaboration is really the best thing we can do for cross-pollination, for growing your audience and helping other people grow their audiences—especially for YouTube, because that's how it works. On YouTube, you find videos by similar creators, so if you have a lot of overlap with this other person's audience, then they will probably eventually see your videos through the algorithm. It needs to be organic, though. There's nothing worse than a collaboration that was very obviously put together by Google SEO. An audience can feel how inorganic it is.

You have to be really careful when [being] approached by people you don't know; try to have a good sense of people. I say no to about ninety-nine out of a hundred requests. The last person I did a collaboration with had a much smaller following at the time, but someone had recommended him to me before, so I knew who he was. When he pitched me, it was on a subject I was already versed and interested in, a subject I was already planning to do something on.

If you're approaching someone you don't know, it's best to have a pitch. And be prepared for that pitch to be rejected, because most pitches are, and that's okay. It's nothing personal, because there are only so many hours in a day and the collaboration needs to work for both parties. If you're going to be in the creative field, you gotta get used to rejection.

What has surprised you about your work?

When I first started in 2008, a twelve-minute video was unheard of. People were like, "Twelve minutes, that's huge!" And now that's considered short. Like I didn't really change my format, but my profile started to rise when the algorithm shifted toward longer-form [videos]. I just got lucky, and YouTube started trending in favor of longer videos with high engagement rates.

I guess it was a surprise that eventually doing what you do could eventually pay off, not because you were good but because the algorithm deemed your length and engagement the right combination to recommend other people [to] your videos.

What tool could you not do without?

Assistants [laughs]. I have my co-writer and editor, Angelina; I have Antonella, who does my finances; and I have Eliza, who takes care of my Patreon and monitors my comments.

Are there any particular obstacles you've overcome to get where you are?

The problem with the narrative of any creator is the idea that you've overcome things. I can't think of anything I've overcome. I could say imposter syndrome, but the truth is I live with that constantly. Most things are just kind of things I didn't get over; I just learned to live with [them].

As someone who has been an online content creator for more than ten years, how do you feel audiences have changed over time?

The truth is, [audiences have] gotten worse since I started. At first I was like, "It can only get better from here," but the truth is the longer I've done this, the worse the comments get, the worse the harassment gets. You just get used to it. I know that sounds terrible. It's why I don't look at comments anymore, I don't look at Twitter mentions anymore, I do not search myself, I don't go on Reddit. In order to stay sane, I have to focus on the work and not the feedback, and that's become a necessity. The truth is you just get used to it; you have to live with it. So I wouldn't say I've overcome things. I've figured out how to live with it because it's, uh, not great.

Who are your inspirations?

[There] was a segment on a show on Current TV called "Target Women," and it was hosted by a woman named Sarah Haskins. She's kind of a proto–Jenny Nicholson, if you will, only she didn't talk about Star Wars; she talked about ads targeted at women, and in terms of actual Internet content, I would say she was my first real inspiration. I wanted to make real, cutting, pithy videos where the media I was talking about kind of spoke for itself, and she was really, really good at that.

There are other writers, too. Film Crit Hulk—I've bagged on him in my videos, but his style of writing, like the sort of empathic approach he takes to film writing. Todd VanDerWerff, too; he did work for the AV club [and] now he works for Vox. com. Nowadays I feel like I take the most inspiration from people who do what I do—people like Becky Newman and Dan Olsen and ContraPoints and hbomberguy and Jenny Nicholson and

Captain Disillusion. [Captain Disillusio's] got one of my favorite YouTube channels, because he never follows the same formula even though he talks about the same topic. I think seeing your peers always trying to raise the bar makes you want to do the same. That's one area I feel lucky about right now, I feel like I'm in a place where I really respect my peers and they're an inspiration, and I think that speaks to how far video essays have come as a medium—that there's a validity building and we can inspire one another.

What tips would you offer newcomers to this industry?

Since I've been doing this for so long [and] the industry changes so differently from year to year, I'm gonna borrow what Contra-Points said fairly recently: You need to pay close attention to the conversation you want to be a part of and figure out the thing that's not being said and the perspective that's not saying it. Since [video essays are] a visual medium, you need to figure out a way to make yourself visually distinct from everybody else. The people who fail tend to be the people who are just aping what's already there. There is a box, because people like what they like, but they also like new stuff, so stick a foot outside of the box and have a keen sense of what your tone is and who you are and what your personality is. People like personality. Going off and being bland and trying to play to what you think people want to hear? People sniff that out immediately and tend to get really bored by it.

[Corporate buyouts] happens all the time in this industry. Current TV was a tragedy because it got bought out by Al Jazeera America, which then disappeared. The same thing happened to Blip.TV—it got bought out by Maker [Studios] and then Maker got dissolved and now Blip is just gone and it's a complete waste. I'm kind of waiting for the other shoe to drop with Patreon. I'm like, "Patreon's gonna get bought out and then it's gonna be Blip all over again." So hoard your nuts, squirrels!

CLIMBING THE TOWER OF VIEWCOUNTS TO REACH THE GOLDEN HEIGHTS OF A METAPHOR I GOT LOST IN

OR

TIPS FOR GETTING MORE VIEWS AND SUBSCRIBERS

Once you're past the Herculean effort it takes to get started on a new project, you'll begin encountering new obstacles, not the least of which is "How the hell do I get people to watch the stuff I'm putting out there?" Well, dear reader, there's no magic formula for increasing viewcounts. There *are* a few things you can do to nudge things in an upward direction, though.

CUT THE WHITE NOISE

Track down and cut out the waste from your video, things like "um," "uh," deep inhales, moments where you're lost in contemplation, burps, sneezes, and pretty much any other type of bodily-expulsion.

KEEP DOWN THE BACKGROUND SOUNDS

If you want people to watch your videos, you'll need to be able to be heard and to cut out typical racket such as fans, loud music, traffic sounds, vociferous animals, and the endless moaning of the undead.

PROMOTE, THEN PROMOTE SOME MORE, THEN PROMOTE SOME MORE AFTER THAT

Be *shameless* in your self-promotion. No one is going to promote your brand as hard and fast as you.*

BE CAREFUL OF YOUR MUSIC

YouTube and other video sites can be *weird* about copyrights, letting entire channels of ripped music go scot-free while striking someone's account

---

* Follow me on Twitter: @rocketllama

because a game's soundtrack was going in the background while they were playing that game. If you want to be a professional, you'll need to play it safe, so try to use music that is either completely original or something in the public domain—i.e., free for everyone to use. Despite what many people seem to think, posting "no copyright infringement intended" in your video description doesn't give you permission to use other people's music (or video) content and can still lead to your stuff getting yanked.

MAKE PERIODIC "BEST-OF" COMPILATIONS

Best-of compilations are the YouTube equivalent of sitcom flashback episodes—they are easy to throw together, make nice money for the cost and effort, and often can draw in new viewers by showing off the best of what you've got. Conversely, unless you're building your videos from contents of livestreams your YouTube audience hasn't all seen, don't make best-ofs too frequently—or your regular viewers will get tired of seeing what amounts to reruns on your channel.

BE CONSISTENT

If there's one thing the Internet likes more than quality, it's consistency. If you're upfront about your posting schedule and stick to it, you will have a far easier time building your subscriber base.

MAKE IT CHEAP

As with any new business, you're not likely to see much of a return on your investment for a while. The lower you keep your early costs, the sooner you'll be able to profit.

BE CLEVER WHEN NAMING YOUR ONLINE VIDEOS

Whether you're naming an online article, a new blog, or a video, keep it *brief*. Short titles that immediately give potential viewers an idea of what your video is about are your best bet; open-ended questions implied to be answered by your video can work, too (unless you don't actually answer the question— because that's clickbait). Do a keyword search for words related to your video to see what's trending that week and build on it. Lastly, keeping your title under sixty characters (give or take a few) makes it easier for it to pop up in search engines.

DESCRIBE THE HELL OUT OF IT

While short titles are best, descriptions are a place you can fill to the brim with information. If someone clicks the full description for a video, they already want to know more, and it's your job to make that as easy as possible. Only a small number of characters are visible in YouTube's search results, so lock in the most critical keywords and URL links to your social networks and website. From there, your description should be filled with things such as links to your other popular/ related videos, friends' channels, alternate channels, and general information about how you made your video and what your channel is about. If someone clicks your video's description, it's your chance to make a regular viewer out of them and keep 'em coming back for entertainment and information.*

SMART TAGS

Tags are the words search engines use to categorize your videos. When you post something, do some research to find the most popular and relevant key-words for that particular video to up its chances of being discovered.

LEARN THE RULES

No matter what style of video content you're making, there will be a set of rules on how to best create and present said content. The time-honored art form of sketch comedy, for example, has a whole slew of rules you should know. There's the rule of three, which states that three beats of a gag should end with the third being an unexpected variation of the gag for maximum impact.† Then there's the rule of the question, which states that a good way to end a sketch is with an unexpected answer to the *who, what, where, why,* or *when* of a situation. And the rule of heightening, which states that you need to heighten

---

* While it was previously considered a no-no, it's become quite common for video descriptions to have links to products and affiliates to make the content creator some advertising money.
† There's also the lesser-used rules such as the rule of five, which employs five comedy beats rather than three, and the *Family Guy* rule, where you repeat a joke endlessly until all humor has left it and your life.

the situation somehow during the sketch, rather than simply maintaining the same level of comedic tension. And the rule of space, which states that you should *never* heighten a joke until it goes to space, because it shows you've run out of ideas on how to heighten the situation and have settled for the obvious maximum.

See? That's a lot of rules, and I've barely scratched the surface of what it takes to make a single type of video. Whatever your genre, if you want to make something worth watching, it's going to take some serious study.

WATCH FOR STOLEN CONTENT

Now, hopefully you're not the kind of person who would stoop to stealing other people's content (and if you are, *knock it off, dick!*). However, the dusky shadow of content theft will still loom large over you in the form of other people taking what you've made and trying to profit from it themselves. YouTube and other big video sites generally have quick and painless reporting systems, though they're not flawless in terms of speed and effectiveness. Your best bet is going to be to keep an eye on your stuff by doing periodic searches of your own videos and related keywords.

There also may be times where larger channels and brands ask to repost your work, like if you get a popular YouTube video, they might repost it on Facebook with some kind of giant caption telling people how they should feel about it. You know, "THIS IS SO PERFECT!" or "OMG SO CUTE I CAN'T EVEN!" or "WAIT FOR BATMAN," that sort of thing. Rarely, they'll offer to pay you, which can be a nice deal to take (although it should only be taken if they pay you and give you full credit/link to your page, otherwise it's not going to build your brand at all).

Often, though, you'll get the much crummier offer to have your stuff reposted in exchange for the exposure you'll get. This . . . is a bad deal. They're going to make money off your work under the guise of helping you build your brand, and whatever exposure you're going to get is likely going to be minuscule compared to what they're going to get. Remember: These big channels are not your friends, they're companies who want to make money. Don't let yourself get screwed over in the interest of being polite or gaining exposure. Exposure bucks won't keep the lights on.

YOU NEVER KNOW WHAT WILL OR WON'T TAKE OFF

Sir Sean "*Zardoz*" Connery passed on both *The Lord of the Rings* and *The Matrix* because he didn't enjoy or understand them and didn't think they'd do well. When he got the chance to do *The League of Extraordinary Gentlemen*, he didn't understand it, either, so he jumped on it under the assumption it would be the hit that would make up for his past misses. It was not.

Much like Sir Connery, you never know what will or won't do well. There might be a video you pour your heart and soul into but that only gets a paltry number of hits, and there might be something stupid that you hate but you post it anyway and it's what busts your channel wide open. Whether something is your big break or not is largely out of your control; the only thing you can control is what you're putting out there (so make it really good).

TOP EIGHT OMG REALLY GOOD WAYS TO GET VIDEO HITS YOU WON'T BELIEVE

(#3 MADE US FEEL ALL THE FEELS IN OUR FEELGLANDS)

1 All your video thumbnails should contain suggestive imagery, like a frame of a woman who looks like she's undressing, or an image of a woman with a CENSORED bar across her breasts despite the fact she's fully clothed.

2 Make a stupid face in every thumbnail. A combination of *JOY / AGONY / PRE-VOMIT* is the best.

3 Abuse keywords and hashtags even if it's misleading. *#BLESSED #LIFEHACK #ONEDIRECTIONNUDEPARKOUR #FREETACOS*

4 Hop on every trend and meme even if you hate and don't understand them. You can find more about this by purchasing my *GRUMPY CAT FIDGET SPINNER ONLY '90S KIDS NOSTALGIA DLC PACK.*

5 MAKE ALL TITLES IN ALL-CAPS ALL THE TIME AND **IF YOU CAN BOLD IT, TOO, YOU SHOULD**

6 *BUY ALL YOUR VIEWERS DESPITE IT BEING ILLEGAL AND POTENTIALLY GETTING YOUR CHANNEL BANNED.*

7 *GET A DOUCHEY HAIRCUT.*

8 *HAVE A DOUCHEY FACE.*

9 **SEND ME ALL YOUR MONEY.**

THE TRICKLE OF THE TREASURE TROVE: WHAT TO DO ABOUT INCOME

One of the most important things you can do for your channel is to figure out your finances early. When making a nerdy living, it takes a while to get money to trickle in. Once it does, however, you may find that your friends, who didn't mind helping out for free, are suddenly going full *Leprechaun 4: In Space* and screaming at you about their pot o' gold.

You'll need to not be selfish, yet also not let other people run all over you. Your friends and family are investing their time and effort into helping out. Even in the early days when you're broke, show your appreciation for your helpers with the judicious application of pizza. When the money starts to arrive, have a talk with the team to get a feel for their expectations. If you're working with someone whose thoughts and ideas are critical to your channel or project, someone who puts in the same time and energy as you, then, yeah, split those dang profits. For other helpers with lower levels of investment and effort, find out what other people in similar positions earn (if there are other people in your unique position, which there may not be) and pay them what feels right. Early on, it will probably be so small they won't care about the money itself; they'll simply appreciate that you're not taking them for granted. Once things get really rolling and people are putting in more-or-less full-time efforts and you're getting some real-ass money, pay your people.*

TO SLEEP, PERCHANCE TO STREAM

Though streaming and video-making are heavily interrelated, there are enough differences that not everyone who does one is going to want to do the other. Video editing gives creators time to carefully orchestrate their work; live-streaming rewards spur-of-the-moment thinking and provides a sense of immediacy and intimacy for an audience who is experiencing your content in more-or-less real time.

---

* In the unlikely event you're doing everything alone, you won't have to worry about any of this and can instead keep all your money and go swimming in it like Scrooge McDuck.

Before getting into streaming, you'll need to have some serious chops when it comes to scheduling out your life. A video can be filmed and constructed over the course of several days/weeks/months/years; a live-stream has to happen in a large block of time. Anyone who has tried to get a regular Dungeons & Dragons group together as an adult can attest to how difficult it is to get adults to commit specific blocks in their schedule.

One reason many streamers try to do streams in huge chunks of time is because it helps increase accessibility for audience members in different parts of the world. Australian viewers may want to watch your American stream to listen in bewilderment as you say everything with hard *R*s, or Americans may want to watch your Australian stream to try to decipher the roundabout wordplay of your ripper Australian slang. Trying to reach folks in different time zones is a great way to build an audience, so long as you don't risk your health to do it.

Live-streaming requires severe stamina from you, dear content creator, as you stream for hours on end. This physical demand can be dangerous, as the pressure to succeed can lead streamers to push themselves to deadly degrees. Brian "Poshybrid" Vigneault died in the middle of a twenty-four-hour stream due to complications related to streaming.[16] Joe "Geekdomo" Marino nearly fell victim to a similar fate; like Vigneault, he began experiencing unusual body pains that were signs of a potentially deadly condition. Fortunately, Marino got medical intervention and changed his work and lifestyle habits before fatal damage could occur.[17] Blood clots, heart failure, weight gain, and countless other medical maladies that arise from sitting still for too long are all plausible problems for live-streamers, not to mention that many streamers, in the battle to stay up and "on" for so many hours, will turn to drugs to keep their focus sharp.

This is a career that doesn't lend itself to healthful life choices. If you're streaming alone for eight, twelve, sixteen, or twenty-four hours, you'll be hard-pressed to find time to eat right, exercise, or even go to the bathroom. And, with live-streaming being as new as it is, the industry is very poorly regulated. To stay healthy and alive, it's suggested you do the following:

- **Exercise regularly and eat right.** These tips apply to all humans, *especially* any humans with a sedentary job. When you're streaming, squeeze in exercise where you can, even if it's on camera. Force yourself to hop up and do jumping jacks every time you get a kill, or do push-ups if someone makes a donation to your stream. It's okay to be a little bit of a dancing monkey, because dancing helps keep you alive.

- **Get a cohost or an offscreen helper.** No man is an island, no woman is a wo-island. Despite the additional scheduling difficulties having a cohost/helper brings, having help will make your life infinitely easier in the long run, as it allows you the freedom to take care of common needs like going to the bathroom, eating meals, capturing the screeching baby crawling on the walls and cursing you in demonic tongues, etc. Plus, having to be "on" all the time to perform for your audience will wear you out, so having a cohost will help keep the energy high in times when you need a break. If you don't know any potential cohosts, at the very least you should try to have someone be your offscreen helper. Offscreen helpers aren't going to do much when it comes to hosting duties. They can, however, get you food and water, keep an eye on your health, and maybe keep your stream entertained for a few minutes here and there while you hit the ol' privy.*

- **Plan ahead for long streams.** If you're going to stream for a long period of time, first see a doctor to make sure you're physically up to the challenge. Plan your meals ahead of time so you can eat right while streaming, drink lots of water, and for goodness' sake get some good sleep beforehand.

- **Stream responsibly.** If you begin feeling ill, stop streaming and take care of yourself. No job is worth your life.

---

* Old-timey British for "toilet/bathroom." Modern Brits refer to toilets as *the loo*; Australians might call it a *dunny* if it's outdoors; and in the world of Eberron, they're called *swirling portals of decimation.*

Like any live show, live-streaming is highly vulnerable to technical issues. For example, let's say you were supposed to have a young adult author on to talk about the inspirations for her latest book, but during the stream her AI assistant device wouldn't stop screaming the search results for "Sonic the Hedgehog fanfiction" and the author didn't know how to turn it off, so the whole thing devolved into the two of you shouting over a robot voice babbling about Sonic the Hedgehog's and Shadow the Hedgehog's magical baby. Or, you know, maybe a mic isn't working or something. Ask anyone who's ever done a live show and they'll tell you about the thousand-plus snafus that can and will occur. Having an assistant/cohost can help offset the dead air that would otherwise result from many of these oopsies, but not even the best cohost can stop 'em all, and you know what? That's life. Don't sweat it too hard if technical difficulties smack your channel in the face sometimes.

Even if you do get the technical problems smoothed out and have a regular, healthy streaming schedule, it still may not lead to much income for a while. Making money from live-streams is trickier than from standard YouTube videos. Live-streams don't have as many built-in options for making cash, so you'll have to hustle that much harder for sponsorships, donations, and subscriptions from fans. Fortunately, Internet audiences seem to have an ever-growing understanding of the need for content creators to actually get *paid* for the content they're making if it's to continue, and so they have become increasingly receptive to throwing a few bucks toward their favorite stuff-makers.

IT'S A TOUGH GIG . . . BUT THE TROUBLE'S WORTH IT

Streaming isn't all negatives; far from it. Many fans and creators love the feel of live-streams, as they're intimate ways to interact with (hopefully) cool people online. There are tons of different options for streaming platforms, with Twitch, YouTube, and Facebook Live being a few of the bigger names out there, giving you the power to pick which platform fits your style and maximizes your reach.

Live-streaming is pretty cheap. Since live-streams are, by their nature, *live*, viewers don't expect a lot of ornamentation. You can get by with good sound, decent video, and maybe a picture-in-picture of you as you're playing games/building things/performing music.

Given the inherent difficulty of live-streaming, the medium isn't as crowded . . . in part because the burnout rate for live-streaming is pretty high. Most people are only going to stream for a few weeks, tops, before realizing it's not for them. In this field, your resiliency should pay off (more) quickly.

It's easy to transform live-streamed content to make more money off of it. Do a live-stream, edit that sucker into bite-size shape, and upload it to YouTube, Facebook, Twitter, etc. Maybe even create a blog post to go along with each archived item to talk about the high points of the night's events (a task made easier if you take small notes during the stream to remember when particularly funny, attention-worthy, or potentially meme-able* moments happen).

Live-streaming is a gamer's paradise. Whether you play games of the board or video variety, if you know how to put on a good show, then you may find yourself drawing in the eager viewers. Which isn't to say non-gaming content can't take off—Twitch's "IRL" section dedicated to people streaming their "real life" activities proved to be quite popular when it launched—they're just not as common. Regardless, stream what you want! If you know how to do something cool, stream yourself doing it and hang out with some virtually-connected people.

---

* Yeah, that's right, I wrote the word *meme-able*. It's a meme's world, baby. We're just loling in it.

WAYS TO GROW YOUR AUDIENCE AS A STREAMER

- **Be interactive.** Streaming audiences generally enjoy interactivity. They dig it when streamers thank them for donations and subscriptions, and they enjoy having a conversation about what's going on. There's a reason they are there, watching your live-stream, instead of watching pre-recorded video content—they're there because your live-stream is *live*.

- **Know what you want to get out of streaming.** Are you looking to make friends, pass the time, or build a career? Given that you're reading this book, you're most likely to lean toward the third option. Regardless of your proclivity, figure it out before you get started.

- **Figure out what your "thing" is.** Do you want to be a streamer renowned for your knowledge of the popular-yet-arcane *Warframe*? A streamer known for playing stylishly even if it means losing like a complete goober sometimes? A streamer known for using an overlay to make you look like a sentient hamburger? Whatever your niche may be, carve that sucker out and smoosh yourself into it like it's Amigara Fault and you're a Junji Ito character.

- **Listen to the people.** When others give advice about what they think you could do differently, do better, or what challenges and activities they'd like to see you tackle, listen to them. They're not always going to be right, but you would do well to take their thoughts into consideration.

- **Be consistent.** The Internet prefers regular entertainment more than it prefers good entertainment, so when you can't do both, be consistent.

- **Learn from your favorites.** What do your favorite streamers do differently from you? What sets the top-tier streamers apart from the lower-tier streamers? Watch, listen, take notes, and apply what you've learned to your own performance.

- **Follow games that are trending, but not crowded.** It's easy to see, at a glance, which games make for the most popular streaming, with regulars like *League of Legends* and *Counterstrike* hogging the top spots for years. Their popularity means more people are watching them, but it also means the field is quite crowded. When new games rise through the ranks, take advantage of their popularity while it lasts.

- **Keep people coming back.** Do giveaways, plan multi-part gaming sessions that work toward a massive goal, do whatever you need to do to keep people interested and returning.

- **Monitor trends in naming.** Whether streamers are naming their sessions with long, descriptive titles, pithier titles that lack information, enigmatic questions, or something else altogether, keep an eye on the trends so you can best adjust what you're doing to draw in your audience.

THE NEXT STEP: ONLINE VIDEOS

So you're past the brutal grind of the first few months of live-streaming and video posting. Now you're making teensy-weensy, tiny steps toward building an audience. You feel comfortable on camera, you've got your schedule hammered out, and you're managing to balance life and content creation so your heart isn't on the verge of gumming up and exploding.

Staying the course is a different beast than getting started; with that beast comes an entirely new set of claws, fangs, and fur. If you want to keep moving forward, you'll need to know how to keep things the same while doing it all different.

MIX IT UP

If it's working, stick to it. While you're busy sticking to it, you should also branch out with smaller, experimental content that tries new things. This will help expand your audience reach while providing much-needed variety to keep you from getting burnt out. Try things that are related to your channel theme; if your channel is about your ongoing Dungeons & Dragons sessions, maybe post videos of you and your party playing some D&D-related video games, such as the Capcom beat-em-up *Dungeons & Dragons: Shadows over Mystara*.* If you review decades-old technology, take a visit to a technology museum and interview the curators. If you post videos of yourself wearing gimp costumes in a basement, dancing to mariachi music and singing Disney tunes in falsetto . . . maybe try not being a super-scary weirdo?

Do holiday and event tie-ins, too. Yeah, they can feel gimmicky; still, if you're having fun with it, your audience will, too, so who cares? Stream spooky games for October, explosive content around the Fourth of July, lovey-dovey stuff around Valentine's Day (or hateful antiromantic stuff if you think Valentine's Day sucks), and, naturally, anything nice and quiet for National Save Your Hearing Day.†

As with any nerdy career, stay mindful of the trends and follow them as much as you can. Search engines and hashtags are regrettably influential things that even the most powerful people in the world must bow down to.

LET'S STICK TOGETHER, YEAH YEAH YEAH!

The Internet is a social place, and there's room for everyone. Doing guest spots on other people's channels is a great way to broaden your reach, as is having others do guest spots on your streams. If you and your guest can be physically together, great. If not, hey, it's the Internet, fool! The physical world is for the weak!

---

* Why that game in particular? Because it's freakin' *rad*, that's why.
† May 31, in the unlikely event you didn't already know.

GO TO VIDEO/STREAMER MEETUPS, MEET EXCITING PEOPLE IN THE FLESH*

A quick Google search will reveal countless content creator meetups happening all over the globe. At these meetups you'll encounter every type of creator: The bright-eyed newbie excited about their channel reaching a thousand total views. The burnt-out nineteen-year-old who has already been in the business too long to enjoy it, yet can't bring themselves to quit. The iconoclast whose four million followers watch her weekly live-streams, where she builds robots and raps about history. And, of course, you, dear reader—the cool, smart, nerdy professional who wants to do what they love and have a lovely time doing it.

Most video meetups try to retain the grassroots element, which helps make nerdy careers so enticing. Sure, there are professionals there, but they're not (just) there for the love of money, they're there for the love of what they do. Some meetups are slick, corporate affairs, with hashtagging, buzzword-obsessed business types running around trying desperately to prove they're on your side so they can make money off you somehow. These more corporate events can be very useful, as not *every* corporate type is a bloodsucking fiend (though some of them will likely leave you feeling like you've been slimed). As nerdy careers become more mainstream, so, too, comes the money, and with the money come the suits. Be smart in your dealings with business-y people; they can be a good gateway to making serious cash, but they can also *seriously* pork you over.

LEARN HOW TO CONTEND WITH FAME, FOLLOWERS, AND FANS

Fans are phenomenal, amazing, supportive, fun people . . . most of the time. *Some* fans are fickle assholes who don't want you doing anything other than the specific thing *they* want you to do.

Japanese idols—corporately manufactured pop stars renowned for their wholesome sweetness—are generally forbidden from doing anything as risqué as, say, having a boyfriend. Should it become public knowledge that an

---

* Or in the not-flesh. Some of the best streamers in the world are skeletons. #CheckYourFleshPrivilege

idol is dating someone, they will usually face severe criticism from their obsessive fans, forcing them to give a public apology and likely end their career.

YouTuber "Angry Joe" Vargas posts complex video game reviews that combine in-game footage with green-screened skits and costumed characters. For all his success, Angry Joe found himself becoming Fatigued Joe and needed to slow down the rate at which he was producing this content.[18] He kept other types of content flowing on his channel during this hiatus, and yet many of his followers still weren't happy and took to flooding his videos with nasty comments.

Not all followers are of the "do-as-I-demand-or-I-will-destroy-you" variety. Plenty can be generous-to-a-fault, kind, supportive, and downright cool people. It may often seem the former group are more common than the latter, only because content followers aren't as likely to leave all-caps comments on your work. Still, once you begin gaining a following, you'll experience all types of people, so you need to get a handle on what to expect before they show up at your door with duct tape and a shovel.

To provide you with the most comprehensive guide to the kinds of Internet followers you can expect, I plumbed the depths of some ancient catacombs beneath Chicago to find the definitive guide. Written by Gary Gygax in 1969, this unprinted Dungeons & Dragons manual titled Mordenkainen's Almanac of Internet Deities details what you can expect from the Internet's most archetypal denizens.

AN EXCERPT FROM *MORDENKAINEN'S ALMANAC OF INTERNET DEITIES*:

The Patron Gods of Internet Followers

ZOLOMON THE NORMAL Zolomon is a remarkably average follower. She doesn't obsess over your in-jokes, nor does she rib you for not adhering to a strict update schedule. She'll sit through ads but probably won't back you on Patreon.

EGARTH THE EVER-FICKLE Egarth despises change. Any content that isn't delivered the exact way Egarth thinks it should be delivered will draw his ire, and he's more than willing to let everyone in the multiverse know of his displeasure.

AETH'LAS THE ACTIVE Aeth'las likes to comment, Aeth'las likes to tweet, and Aeth'las is more than happy to throw a few bucks your way. She's a happy, altruistic follower who enjoys your content, likes the interaction, and never overstays her welcome. She wants the Internet to be a fun place and does her best to help keep it fun by supporting her favorite content creators.

CHILLWIND THE GHOST Little is known about Chillwind. What does she want? What does she think about your content? She doesn't rate videos, doesn't comment, doesn't click links. She simply watches and moves on.

FILCH-FINGER THE STALKER Filch-Finger is why you should be *very* careful about how much personal information you reveal in your videos. Mentioning that you live in Georgia in one video from five years ago, referencing your high school mascot in another, tweeting about your dad quitting his job at your town's paper mill . . . while normal fans like Zolomon won't connect these disparate facts, Filch-Finger will. Filch-Finger has serious, untreated mental issues, and once you stop responding to his invasive private messages, he'll take it upon himself to figure out where you live and track you down, whether it's through connecting the dots of your online content or some good ol'-fashioned hacking.*

PHTHAGRETH THE BAFFLED ONE Phthagreth doesn't know how they ended up subscribed to your content; was someone else using their computer? Regardless of how they ended up there, their alien mind is not of this world, and they cannot understand even the most basic concepts you're discussing. Their comments are often unintelligible, dragging down potential intellectual discourse by getting confused fifteen seconds into your video.

HARAPHRIM THE WHITE KNIGHT In the eyes of Haraphrim, you can do no wrong. Haraphrim will defend you against any and all nay-sayers, regardless of whether you're actually right. Sometimes Haraphrim will do it in a way that condescends to you, or he may only be trying to "protect" you because you're female, and he may also let you know he's "not like those other guys." Whether Haraphrim's behavior comes from an antiquated sense of politeness or chauvinistic chivalry is something you'll have to figure out, lest you risk having him transform into his dark alter ego, **HARAPHRIM THE SPURNED**, a former fan turned devoted hater of your content.

TUSKREICH THE TROLL Tuskreich is the youngest of the Internet Deities; some estimate his age to be a mere 1,500 years, others think he's closer to 2,200 years old. Due to a combination of poor social skills, boredom, lack of parental monitoring, and lack of real-life social connections, Tuskreich derives his joy from making others miserable online. His bad behaviors are sometimes as small as a dislike or an asinine comment; on others he'll go bigger by posting hateful counter-content decrying the content of others, doxxing, or swatting.†

---

* D&D jokes aside, cyberstalkers are very real threats. The best ways for you to protect yourself against them are to be *very* careful not to post personal information online, to regularly change your passwords, to keep your antivirus software up to date, to keep your home Internet/Wi-Fi secure, and to make sure your closest friends and family know not to post your information publicly. Conversely, if you're obsessively following someone online, for whatever reason, and it ever occurs to you that it might be crossing the line into cyberstalking, *stop it*. Get some help. You're a good person, and you can do better.
† *Doxxing* refers to publicly posting someone's personal information, like their address. *Swatting* refers to calling in phony police threats on someone, often a video streamer, so they can watch, in real time, as a SWAT team descends on the innocent. While swatting isn't especially common, doxxing is, and both are extremely dangerous, evil things to do to a person. People can and do die from them.

LEARN HOW TO HANDLE CONTROVERSY, TROLLING, AND HATE

At some point, you're probably going to have to face off against the slobbering, acid-mawed beast of controversy. Even "Weird" Al Yankovic, a man so nice he gets permission for his song parodies even though he legally doesn't have to get permission for jack-crap, had to endure the ire of Coolio due to some miscommunications about Al's parody of "Gangsta's Paradise." Kotaku.com's Jason Schrier received *death threats* for having the audacity to report that the game *No Man's Sky* was getting delayed.[19] Yep, a bunch of gamers threatened death to a video game reporter for reporting on video game news—i.e., *doing his exact job.* When the Fine Bros., famous for their many types of "reaction" videos featuring people reacting to things, tried to trademark the concept of a reaction video, their subscriber count plummeted. So did the view count on their subsequent videos. After that, their comment sections became nuclear wastelands of hate, sarcasm, and ironic memes, eventually pushing them to rebrand as FBE to combat the taint on the Fine Bros. name.

Whether you're a kind-hearted goofball musician or someone looking to make a quick buck through trademarks, as your fanbase grows, so, too, will your detractor base. Don't hesitate to ignore (or even disable) the comments; the comments section of any online post is almost invariably a wretched hive of scum and villainy. Your video about the five kids' toys you liked the most when you were a child has somehow had its comments section devolve into an argument over the merits and evils of capitalism. Your review of the PG-rated film *The Little Vampire* (2000) has become the go-to spot for people to loudly proclaim how the Catholic church has been hiding real vampires for years. Somehow, your blog post about assembling a replica of Shepard's N7 *Mass Effect* armor drew in dummies who want to argue that the Earth is flat. You can never know what the talkback section will be like. Ignore the comments where possible and when needed, and full-on disable them if you feel the least bit like things are getting out of hand.*

---

* Speaking of comments, the next time you think about commenting on something, perhaps consider what it would feel like to be on the receiving end of your comment. Maybe only speak up if you feel what you're saying is legitimately helpful or encouraging. There are enough condescending assholes and trolls making noise out there—don't add to it.

While some of you will find the video format enticing, others may find it limiting to focus solely on one thing. Perhaps you prefer a scattershot approach, doing lots of little things simultaneously to see what sticks. You like making videos, but you're more interested in the performance that goes into it, the craftsmanship behind your props and costumes. If this sounds more like you, you may have yourself a case of professional cosplayer.

CHAPTER THREE

COSPLAY

W hat is professional cosplay? Is it wearing costumes to conventions and wandering around with your friends? Doing photo shoots? Making costumes? Doing highly skilled makeup work for other cosplayers? Being a booth babe/beefcake for a company paying you to dress up as their character to show the kids they're "with it" and "one of them" despite their sky-high net worths and decadent lifestyles?

The long and short of it is that being a professional cosplayer entails learning a hodgepodge of cosplay-related skills and making money every disparate way you can. It requires hustle, dedication, and a willingness to pose for a zillion pictures. If you've got the grit to stick it out, there's (some) gold in them thar hills. Before we crack into the world of pro cosplay, however, I should probably address a simpler question.

WHAT IS COSPLAY?

Cosplay, short for *costume play*, is the practice of dressing in costume as a specific character, often while attending a fan convention. Unlike the costumes you'd wear to Mardi Gras, El Dia de los Muertos, or National Pancake Day, cosplaying is about capturing the essence of a specific character more than the essence of an event or culture. These characters are *usually* fictional (though I've seen more than a few bearded dudes dressed as George Lucas or Kevin Smith). Cosplayers often like to act "in character" when interacting with other cosplayers, posing for pictures and reacting to picture requests in a manner reminiscent of the character they're portraying. Gruff Wolverine cosplayers will answer questions with a terse "Sure, bub," Deadpool cosplayers shout about chimichangas, etc. Some even go so far as to adopt the character's persona entirely while in costume and refusing to drop character (if this hasn't been called *method cosplay* before, then I'm coining the term here and now).

THE HISTORY OF COSPLAY

Cosplay's origins stretch back to the beginning of the twentieth century. In 1908, a married couple attended a masquerade party at a Cincinnati skating rink dressed as the then-popular characters Mr. Skygack and Miss Dillpickles. Soon thereafter, a different woman won a costume contest also dressed in Skygack apparel. Fans continued this low-scale, primitive style of cosplay for a few decades, until the first World Science Fiction Convention (aka Worldcon) in 1939, when two people created costumes based on the futuristic pulp artwork of Frank R. Paul. The participants of the next Worldcon held an unofficial masquerade/costume contest, inspiring more fans to dress up as their favorite characters at fan conventions.* [20]

Today the hobby has exploded in popularity; with the increased awareness of geek culture comes increased fandom *and* an increased number of fans willing to put in the blood, sweat, and foam to dress as their fave fictional people.

WHY COSPLAY?

Reality blows sometimes. Cosplay gives a means of escape, letting us spend some time around other people who understand the desire to live in a world with airships and dragons and ancient psychic tandem war elephants or the desire to be someone other than ourselves for a little while. Cosplay is a way to connect with other fans who recognize that you're not just dressed as Dipper Pines from *Gravity Falls*; you're dressed as his clone Tyrone from the

---

* While early cosplay was a free-for-all, after a few specific incidents, conventions placed a universal set of rules to define what constitutes proper cosplay, adding regulations against using food as part of your costume (a rule instated after comix artist Scott Shaw dressed as his character "The Turd," using peanut butter for his costume and causing a big-ass gross mess), as well as regulations banning full nudity (boooooooo).

episode "Double Dipper" who has the exact same appearance save for the number two on his hat.

Cosplay lets us pay tribute to the fictional characters who have touched our lives with their stories, to give ourselves creative and technical challenges to overcome, and to empower ourselves through this fantastic new means of expression, which has only just begun to flourish.

THE THREE PHASES OF COSPLAY

Most costumed pros don't start off sanding and soldering their outfits together; they work their way up to it. Expert cosplay scientists[*] have conducted years of painstaking research[†] and determined the three distinct phases[‡] to this art form, found below.

PHASE ONE: CLOSET COSPLAY

Here we have the most basic way to cosplay, which involves using mostly clothes you already own. Common examples include *Daily Bugle* Peter Parker, where you walk around with a camera, regular clothes, and a Spider-Man shirt with the emblem exposed from beneath your overshirt, or *Daily Planet* Clark Kent, which is the same thing but with glasses, a Superman shirt, and that swirly piece of hair in front of your face. This is a low-cost, low-commitment way to dip your toe into the cosplay pool to see if it's something you want to swim around in.

PHASE TWO: PRE-MADE COSPLAY

Here your hunger for cosplay grows beyond the constraints of your closet. Now you want to cosplay as more ostentatious characters, a desire that begets ostentatious purchases. Sometimes you can buy complete costumes as you would for Halloween; others, you'll have to search for the different pieces—a harness here, a set of gun holsters there, leather leggings elsewhere—and merge them all together to assemble the look you want.

---

[*] i.e., me
[†] i.e., going to a lot of conventions
[‡] i.e., three is a nice round number

PHASE THREE: CRAFTED COSPLAY

There's no stopping you now. By the light of each full moon, your insatiable drive to cosplay has become stronger, burning your veins with the *need* to *become*. Now you're not only buying pieces of your costumes, you're buying pieces of things to turn *into* pieces of your costume because nothing in the shops looks right. The shoulder pads are too small, the emblem isn't the right color, and the gun blade is neither gunny nor bladey enough. So you build, abandoning yourself to the art of the cosplay. Weeks go by where you don't speak to another human being. Your friends and family are worried; or at least, their texts and voice mails *sound* worried. Little do they realize that you don't need them anymore. Thread, fabric, foam, glue; these are your family now.

STARTING POINT: STYLES OF COSPLAY

Now that you've abandoned the need for your fellow meatbags, let's talk about cosplay styles. Each cosplay style brings its own expectations with it; while cosplayers have plenty of flexibility to bounce from one genre to another, you should do some research before jumping into a new cosplay style you're not familiar with.

SUPERHERO

- ◆ **PROS:** Superheroes are easily recognizable, their masks provide anonymity that make it more comfortable to stay in character, and the costumes are easy to get.
- ◆ **CONS:** Default superhero costumes leave little to the imagination, so if you don't want your love handles or genitals on full display you'll either want to do some customization or be prepared to spend the day discreetly tugging things into place.

ANIME

- **PROS**: Anime fans are often a wild and accepting bunch, so cosplaying as your favorite anime character is an easy way of meeting excitable new people, and some anime cosplay can be accomplished with something as simple as a blazer and a wig.

- **CONS**: Hair and weapons. Anime characters tend to have bizarrely ornate hair, which doesn't always translate well to real life, and carry comically oversize weapons, which are a pain in the ass to haul around.

SCIENCE FICTION

- **PROS**: Sci-fi properties tend to give you a wide range of difficulty as far as costume creation/selection, so it's easier for cosplayers of all skill levels to find a character whose outfit matches their skills.

- **CONS**: Some of the more recognizable costumes, such as, say, *Star Trek*'s Borg, are a surprisingly big hassle to assemble. Also, there's a small, loud subset of sci-fi fans who are particularly prickly about the presentation of their favorite franchises, and they may be more inclined to explain to you in great detail what they feel are inaccuracies.

FANTASY

- **PROS**: Leather armor, a dagger, and pointed ears, and you're done!
- **CONS**: Fantasy costumes for the guys tend to be suffocatingly hot and heavy in the hubbub of a convention. Fantasy costumes for women, on the other hand, tend to be more revealing than you may be comfortable with. As always, modify those costumes until they look and feel right.

LITERARY

- **PROS:** Cosplaying as characters from literature gives you a bit more freedom to interpret them, as their individual looks are more up to the reader's imagination.

- **CONS:** Don't expect to get recognized as often. With that freedom of interpretation comes a lack of recognizability. The way you imagine Rincewind the Wizard might be antithetical to the way someone else imagines Rincewind.

STEAMPUNK

- **PROS:** If you want to go steampunk, it can be as easy as slapping a few cogs on a leather bustier and grabbing a top hat.

- **CONS:** Steampunk often involves dressing in layers—layers that become very, very hot amidst the hustlin', bustlin' convention floor. Clever steampunk takes on popular characters can be hard to recognize, leading to confused faces from would-be fans.

POST-APOCALYPTIC

- **PROS:** Since your outfit is supposed to be that of someone living in a post-apocalypse world, it's generally pretty hard to go wrong. Throw on some dirt, rip some holes in your clothes, and don't worry about wear and tear on your costume since it's *supposed* to look beat-up.

- **CONS:** It can be difficult to concisely convey your character using roughed-up, cobbled-together costumes, so don't be surprised if you get a lot of looks from people trying to figure out who the hell you are.

FURRY

- **PROS**: Utter anonymity, fuzziness

- **CONS**: The furry crowd is a . . . complicated populace. Some are simply folks who like to express themselves through primal, animal alter-egos. Others like to express themselves *sexually* as these alter-egos. Others still like to express themselves as even more niche, fetishized versions of these alter-egos, engaging in fetishes that I will not be listing because they're gross and/or illegal. There's a fair amount of crossover between these three groups, which has led many non-furries to lump them all together. So if you dress in a costume that someone might consider "furry," don't be surprised if others make some assumptions about your sexual appetites. Also, those giant animal costumes are probably hot as hell unless you get a really fancy one with a built-in air conditioner and butler.

WORDS FROM WORKING NERDS

OhMy!Sophii, professional cosplayer, creator, and social media marketer

I started cosplaying for fun in 2009 when my best friend Cissa took me to A-Kon in Dallas. In 2014 I was fortunate enough to begin working with Ichico Comics. At conventions, it was my job to promote their work while in cosplay. This really helped me break into new and bigger opportunities.

On average, how long does it take for you to complete a project, start to finish?

It really depends on the project. Some cosplay projects take a day or two while others can take weeks. It also depends on what my convention schedule looks like. I typically guest at one or two conventions a month, and I like to have at least one new cosplay for each whenever possible. If I know I have a convention coming up, I'll work on a costume for twelve to fifteen hours each day to get it done. However, if I have no events upcoming for the rest of the month, I'm able to take my time and spread the project out over a week or two.

How important is it for professional content creators to utilize social media?

INCREDIBLY IMPORTANT. I am a huge advocate for social media. At conventions and at home, I dedicate time to teaching people from varying industries how to use social media to their advantage without spending money. This is something I'm very passionate about.

How important do you feel fan conventions are for your line of work?

Top priority. Building the cosplays is, of course, a huge priority; but being able to meet and connect with fellow creators, building community, and networking are the backbone of cosplay. There would be no creators without the fans who adore them.

What tool or material do you enjoy working with the least?

I'm not a big fan of thermal plastics when making armor. It's expensive, and foam can do about everything thermal plastics can, with some exceptions.

What's something you think more people should know or understand about professional cosplay?

I think there's a huge misconception about what "professional cosplay" is, and while I do think it can be defined several ways—guesting, modeling, etc.—I think that regardless of what your professional cosplay venture is, it's not easy. It's hard work, it's a job. If you love what you're doing, if you love your art, then never expect it to come easy. It's worth every minute!

What has surprised you the most about your line of work?

The impact it makes. I started cosplaying for me, because it was fun! Gradually it evolved into a full-time job, and one day I'm at a convention, run into a member of the online community I run—CosLadies Community—and she thanks me for my positivity and explains what an impact I've made on her. That was so powerful. That changed everything about what I do. I realized I'm not cosplaying just for me anymore, I'm cosplaying for my community, and how I carry myself and my work really matters.

What tips might you recommend to newcomers looking to get into the business?

Love what you do, don't get bogged down by anyone else's opinion, and keep doing what you love!

THE NEXT STEP: THINGS YOU SHOULD KNOW WHETHER YOU'RE COSWORKING OR COSPLAYING

No matter your reason for cosplaying, whether it be to promote your other work, to increase your online influence, or as an end unto itself, here are some tips with which cosplayers of all levels of skill and professionalism should become acquainted.

COSPLAY OF A DIFFERENT COLOR (OR GENDER, OR ABILITY, OR . . .)

Don't let anything hold you back from cosplaying who you want. The cosplay community is very welcoming, and fans are usually excited to see clever and heartfelt depictions of beloved characters; so no matter what your circumstance, be who you want to be in cosplay and in life.

COSPLAY ISN'T CONSENT

Just because you're dressed in a skintight suit doesn't mean strangers have the right to run their hands all over you, and, similarly, just because someone is dressed in a way you find sexy doesn't mean you can touch them as you please. If you're not sure how to behave, follow Anne Victoria Clark's quick behavioral guideline: The Rock Test.[21] When interacting with cosplayers, especially female cosplayers, behave toward them with the same mix of admiration, fear, and respect as you would Dwayne "The Rock" Johnson. Would you make lascivious comments toward The Rock about his choice of clothing, or roam your hands over his body when posing for a picture? No, you would not, as he would end your universe for such uncouth behavior. When in doubt, be respectful and help make sure everyone has a good time, dang!

GET READY TO GET HOT AND TIRED

Costumes are usually hotter and more exhausting than you'd expect. On days you plan to cosplay, prepare accordingly by having your friends or servant droids carry extra water for you and by taking breaks when necessary.

BRING A HANDLER FOR BIG COSTUMES

If you're cosplaying as an oversize character, you're probably not going to be able to see or maneuver as well as you're used to. In these situations, it's downright crucial to have a buddy with you to help watch where you're going so you don't bump into people, break things, or take a tumble that destroys your costume.

BRING COSTUME REPAIR KITS

Conventions are exciting places, and sometimes excitement leads to damaged costumes. Plan ahead with a basic repair kit so you can fix minor tears and scrapes. Recommended items include: small scissors with round tips so you don't inadvertently jab a hole in your costume or get accosted by security, hot glue guns and glue sticks, clear nail polish, fabric tape, electrical tape, Velcro, safety pins, bobby pins, hairspray, cotton swabs, super glue, stain removers (bleach pens and the like), needle and thread, bandages for the inevitable blisters, and, if all else fails, the almighty duct tape.

BRING BODY REPAIR KITS

Your makeup might smear, your eyes may dry out, and all that *Halo* armor might start to get a bit funky after a while. Keep a supply of extra makeup, eyedrops, deodorant, bandages, and food/water on hand. Both body and costume repair kits can often be incorporated into your costume with the use of pouches, bags, and deep pockets.

COSPLAY OFTEN

Professional cosplayers cosplay twice a month or more. This will be something you'll have to work up to, as that's not going to be feasible when you're new to the scene—you'd burn through a dragon's hoard of gold trying to pay for all the travel, accommodations, and convention passes. Speaking of which . . .

FIND WAYS OF GETTING TO CONVENTIONS CHEAPLY (OR FOR FREE!)

If you want to cosplay often enough to be a pro, you'll have to cosplay smart, finding ways to get to conventions at little cost. For travel, well, driving is much cheaper than most other forms of transportation, so get used to going by car when possible.

Sometimes you'll want to go to nearby conventions even when they're dinky. Other times, the larger conventions are such good opportunities that it's worth the extra cost. The return on your investment of money and effort will vary from con to con (and year to year), so knowing where to go will take a bit of experience and word-of-mouth from your growing network of convention-going friends.

As far as convention passes go, there are several ways to net those bad boys *gratis*. Firstly, you can volunteer at conventions, as big shows are always looking for friendly people to boss around convention-goers going down the wrong hallway or sitting in the no-sitting areas.

You can also register as a member of the press or as a professional. Press credentials can be earned through avenues such as blogging, vlogging, or working for some kind of actual primitive *paper* publication. Professional badges can be acquired through a number of different ways, not the least of which is submitting panels and having them accepted. Panels generally require you to have your crap together and to know enough people who have *their* crap together *and* to be creative about the topics you're presenting to an audience of convention-goers who are electing to spend their valuable time with you. Go to panels you find interesting, take notes on how they were organized, and, above all, *talk to people*. Being social is an important part of being a professional nerd, no matter your particular specialty. Talk to your fellow conventurers while waiting in line, talk to panelists after their panels, talk to the people working booths—talk to everyone!*

There are plenty of real-life benefits to meeting new people, such as making flesh-and-blood friends and getting flesh-and-blood dates.† On the business side of things, networking is a huge part of professional nerdiness. Find other like-minded professionals and make plans to work with them. Maybe connect with someone who has a YouTube series you can guest-appear on as whatever character/costume you're trying to promote, or find a relatively new photographer who needs practice doing shoots. Cooperation isn't just the nice thing to do, it's the *smart* thing to do.

---

* Or, should I say, talk to everyone politely, without being creepy or rambling or lingering awkwardly.
† No offense to any mummies. I'm sure you're plenty dateable.

WORDS FROM WORKING NERDS

Ginny Di, content creator, Internet personality, and professional cosplayer

On average, how long does it take for you to complete a project, start to finish?

It totally depends on the project. I have costumes I've made in a matter of hours, and there's even a music video I made in under a week from concept to release. I also have costumes I've worked on for six months and music videos that took months to plan, prepare for, film, edit, and release. Most of my costumes are completed in under a month, but sometimes that's twenty hours of work and sometimes that's 100 hours of work. Sometimes a photoshoot is one hour of shooting and two hours of editing for the whole set, other times (like my Harry Potter pinup photo sets) it's days of shooting and two hours of editing per photo. I like to intersperse quick, light projects with big, complex projects when possible.

Monetization is the key issue for many creative types; how do you find the funds to pursue your passion?

I think the biggest key to making money as a cosplayer (or any creative) is to recognize that sometimes the most lucrative things you can start doing are things no one can tell you to do. By the time you're hearing about Patreon, everyone is doing Patreon and it's getting harder to make money off it. By the time you learn about people selling Polaroids or cosplay construction walkthrough PDFs, there are already people selling to that market. The best thing you can do is come up with the *next* Patreon, or Polaroids, or PDFs. What can you do that's unique? What can you offer that no one else is offering yet? Some trends are useful to follow, but you have to be ready to think up the next trend if you want to stop playing catch-up and actually start getting ahead.

In addition to professional cosplay, you're also a blogger and YouTuber, among other things. What do you feel are the advantages of pursuing your passions from more than one angle, as opposed to putting all your efforts into a single avenue?

There's been some talk lately about the "cosplay bubble" and about how it may burst soon. That is to say, cosplay might be a profession now, but it's extremely new, and that industry that sprang up practically overnight could collapse overnight, too. We're reaching a point of saturation where it's easier than it's ever been before to be an amazing cosplayer—you can buy commercial patterns for practically anything, cosplay fabrics are sold in your local JoAnn's, you can shoot beautiful cosplay photos on your iPhone, you can buy thermoplastics and 3-D printers with pocket money. While that accessibility is great for hobbyists, it's dangerous for professionals, because what makes us unique and valuable is becoming less and less unique and valuable. By the same token, any field can disappear without warning—YouTube's changes to advertising features had some YouTubers losing as much as 90 percent of their revenue, for example. For me, involving myself in more than one "field" leaves me flexible, so if YouTube disappears, or cosplay stops being popular, I don't have to restructure my entire business. It also gives me room to reshuffle if my interests change.

What's something you think more people should know or understand about professional cosplay?

It's so much more than just putting on a costume and looking pretty. A professional cosplayer is a small business owner—we don't just do the actual cosplay, we negotiate appearances, manage merchandise production and sales, and do our own accounting, branding, and marketing. If it was just about looking nice in a costume, there would be a lot more professional cosplayers than there actually are.

What are your favorite and least favorite tools and materials to work with?

For actual cosplay construction, I couldn't do it without my seam ripper, which sounds counter-intuitive—a seam ripper is for taking out seams, not putting them in. With every single costume, I make mistakes, and being prepared to backtrack and try again is absolutely imperative, not just to ending up with a great final product but to learning and growing as a craftsperson.

I hate dyeing fabric, although I do it a lot. I hate that there are no take-backs, so if you mess up, you've wasted a ton of money and time and you need to buy all new fabric and start again. Dyeing is more art than science, so even though I've done it a half-dozen times now for costumes, I still get nervous each time, and each attempt feels equally unpredictable.

What tips might you recommend to newcomers looking to get into the business?

Treat it as a serious hobby before you even think about treating it like a business. Managing a small business is hard, existing in the public eye and getting hate and harassment is hard, motivating yourself to work when you could lie in bed and watch Netflix and no one would stop you is *hard*. It's only worth it if you really, truly love what you're doing. Keep your day job, and spend a year or two taking your cosplay/YouTube/creative hobby *very* seriously first. See how it goes, see how hard it is to make money and to grow, see what you love about it and what you hate, and only *then* should you start to think about it as a potential career.

I used to think this kind of work was all about raw talent, but I've learned firsthand that it's actually mostly about how many hours, how much sweat, you're willing to put into it.

HOW TO EARN SWEET LOOT WHILE DRESSED AS AMBUSH BUG: MAKING MONEY COSPLAYING

Now that you know some more about how to cosplay, you're probably wondering how to make *money* cosplaying. Well, it should be pretty obvious, you have to . . . well, you sell . . . hmm . . .

As it turns out, being a pro cosplayer is *hard*, much harder than many of the other career paths in this book. If you want to do it, you've got to have dedication and a willingness to try different things.

PRINT SALES

As you might expect, this is where you print out nice, glossy pictures of your costumes to sign and sell at cons. While this is a type of revenue previously restricted to celebrities and their ilk, that's no longer so today. Highly skilled photographers and costumers alike have helped legitimize and popularize print sales, and they are now a mainstay of any pro cosplayer. Print sales' biggest weakness is that you're unlikely to get many repeat sales, since people will generally only buy a single picture at a time, and they're certainly not going to buy more than one of the same picture. As you continue working and expanding your photo arsenal, it will become easier to sell more than one print per customer, but there's still a soft limit to how many pics the average person is willing to buy.

ENTER CONTESTS AT CONVENTIONS

Costume contests are, for some pro cosplayers, the chance to *really* strut their stuff. Some contests have big cash prizes that will go well beyond the cost of building your entry. Others might offer a plastic trophy. Regardless of what the prize is, doing well in a costume contest will raise your brand and give you something to list as a credential. Costume contests have become relatively common at larger conventions and generally have a specific set of rules judges will base their decisions on regarding whose cosplay rocks it the most.[22]

- **Accuracy:** how accurate your portrayal is to the character you're portraying. It can be little things like picking the right shade of blue for Nightcrawler's fur, or making sure you have the right number of glowing wing-tentacles for your *Diablo II* Tyrael armor.

- **Construction:** how well you've made your costume. Can you move in it? Does it stay together as you move around? Did you use a variety of materials and techniques to give your costume more dimension than simple foam and spray paint?

- **Presentation:** This is where your ability to ham it up comes into play. If you can fully commit to a character by talking like them, walking like them, and spitting out catchphrases like them, you're going to wow judges and the audience alike while also probably having a pretty rad time. Group contest entries, such as those who perform skits or dances, will often score big here.

- **Audience impact:** how much do the people like you? Your costume may not be the most technically accomplished or your impression the most accurate, but if you've got the spark that lights the crowd ablaze with excitement, you might be able to pull out a win (or, at the very least, an honorable mention).

VLOGGING/YOUTUBE SERIES

Running a vlog is an excellent way for pro cosplayers to earn some extra income and attention. Vlogs give you a platform to give other cosplayers tips and ideas for their own creations, they're generally easy to monetize, and they can be a good way to let off some steam and express yourself. *Plus* having an established YouTube presence raises the likelihood you'll get asked to do collaborations with other YouTubers, upping your overall presence and hopefully having some fun in the process.

SPONSORED COSPLAY

Sponsored cosplay, also known as being a booth babe/beefcake, is when you're paid by a company to dress as one of their characters to help promote them. Such opportunities are infrequent but pay quite handsomely.

USE SUBSCRIPTIONS AND ONLINE MARKETPLACES TO SELL FULL TUTORIALS FOR COMPLETE COSTUMES

Once you've completed your latest bomb-ass costume, sell the step-by-step instructions for how others can make the same costume, either as a video walkthrough or a PDF or an Excel file or whatever format fits your work best. Tutorials make for great content to offer subscribers, and there's basically no financial cost to creating them since you're merely cataloguing the things you're already doing. The only real cost is that it will take some extra time to pay extra attention to what you're doing and to take notes on each step.

SHARE SALES

Become an associate of an online business such as Amazon or Groupon and, in the body of YouTube videos, blog posts, or Instagram photos, tuck in your associate information. This way, if someone uses one of those online services, you'll get a little bit of referral money (at no cost to them). It's small, but it can add up.

STRAIGHT-UP ADVERTISING

Stick at it long enough, and your posts and videos will get sponsorship offers from companies looking to advertise. Before accepting (or even responding to) their offers, do some research on the company to make sure they're reputable. You don't want to tarnish your image by advertising some sleazy fly-by-night pyramid scheme or sexy tank-battle game for the iPhone. Remember: Even if the money is good, if you're not comfortable doing something, *don't*.

SELL YOUR COSTUMES

If you aren't too attached to a costume, put it up for sale. If it was a particularly complicated build, don't be afraid to ask for more money with the knowledge that there's an ever-moving sweet spot for pricing items like this. Charge too little, and people will think it's not worth very much. Charge too much, and people won't be able to afford it.

CREATE A BRAND OF COSPLAY ITEMS

Once you're *really* far along, you may be able to turn your personal brand into a line of products, licensing out your name and image for cosplay supplies. This doesn't happen often, but when it does it means a nice treasure trove for adventurous cosplayers.

> "[Making money as a professional cosplayer] is NOT EASY. I work more hours doing cosplay full-time than I did at my forty-hour-a-week factory job. I'm always thinking about what I need to be doing, planning for my next event or project, while working on current projects and editing photos from previous ones. I feel every emotion there is to feel, I mess up, I have good weeks and bad weeks. I have to work for every penny. I don't just sit around looking pretty at my sewing machine, raking in the cash like some people assume. It's intense work, but it's extremely rewarding.
>
> "I wish I could help people understand that there's no magic formula for success. It's not just 'make stuff and post photos,' and it's not 'do lingerie shoots and open a Patreon.' It's SO much more than that."
>
> —April Gloria, professional cosplayer

After all this, you may find you're not as interested in wearing your costumes as you are making them. Or perhaps you're not even especially interested in making costumes; rather, you want to make various nerdy items that please the four corners of your soul. If that's the case, you should look into becoming a professional crafter.

CHAPTER FOUR

CRAFTING

Of the many nerdy careers discussed in this book, crafting might be the easiest one to explain to your less-than-nerdy relatives. If you're making something tangible, something a person can look at and feel and hold, it's easier for them to wrap their minds around how you're making a living. That said, they still might not understand why people are shelling out money for your *Lord of the Rings* replica weapons or hand-knitted Princess Zelda dresses, but at least they won't constantly ask what you're doing with your time.

STARTING POINT: CRAFTING CRAFTABLE CRAFTS

Crafting is for the tactile-minded geek—those of us who like to hold a problem in our hands and know that those same hands can find a solution. It's not for the faint of heart, as it requires a higher tolerance for filth, rough edges, and an ever-expanding workspace.

Many crafters get into the career for the same reason—they like building things. They start small, painting pewter statues in their garage or crocheting to keep their hands busy while they watch TV. Soon they find their interest expanding, their minds drifting back to building when they're doing other things. That's when it's too late to resist the call; you've already been chosen by The Craft.

CHOOSING YOUR CRAFT

The types of craftables you can work with will be very contingent on the amount of space at your disposal. If you live in an apartment, for example, it's going to be tough to get the room required to weld realistic replicas of the Iron Throne, not to mention the high risk of a stray spark creating a *Towering Inferno*-type situation in your complex. Even easier-to-handle crafts like crochet can take up serious space, so know that, regardless of what you choose, supply storage will be something you need. In these situations, plastic tubs are your best friend. Maybe in other situations, too. I've known a few folks whose best friend was a tub.

If you want to minimize clutter, making wearables—common items of clothing like scarves, jackets, and jewelry—is your best bet. While spools of yarn can be gregarious, they don't make messes composed of foam particles or stray shards of metal.

Custom figurines rate somewhat higher on the untidiness scale than wearables. A good table will probably be enough to contain the various paint and glue spatters, so long as you're diligent about them.

Larger items such as weapon and armor replicas, furniture, and all forms of geek home decor generally require a high cost of entry and a higher tolerance for making messes. You'll need more space to work, more space for the larger materials, and to spend considerably more to get the custom tools needed. They also have a higher cost of failure; so if this is the market you're going for, you'll want to do additional research before launching into a big build—you don't want to spend two months making something no one wants to buy. Also, larger materials are typically more expensive to replace, so you'll need to be careful and have plenty of backups for when the inevitable boner* occurs.

CHOOSE THE RIGHT TOOLS

Doing something as small-scale as painted custom figures will be easier if you have a variety of brushes at your disposal; trying to use the same brushes you

---

* I'll have you know the term *boner* means a goof-up or mistake. I don't know *why* you're chuckling.

painted the house with will be an outrageous waste of your time. If you're going to spend the time and effort and money to start up something like this, it's worth doing right, so buy the correct tools for the job.

GO NUTS ON SALES, BUT DON'T GO *TOO* NUTS
It's all too easy to impulse-buy supplies. You're at the store anyway; why not grab some supplies? Or maybe Amazon is having a nice sale on yarn, so why not get enough yarn to last you through the next few years? Because your needs may change before you get a chance to use all the crafting materials you impulse-purchased, that's why. Plus the more extra materials you have stowed away, the more likely they'll get damaged before you get the opportunity to use them. When purchasing materials, purchase them with a plan in mind, not just because they're there.

RECORD YOUR WORK
Since you're going to be spending your time crafting anyway, do a video channel or pictographic blog post to accompany major projects, either of which could work as a supplementary source of income or a reward for your paid subscribers. If you don't want your face or voice on camera, you can record just your hands and add captions to keep things nice and depersonalized.

PRACTICE!
Dedicate time and energy toward practicing in a low-pressure environment. Buy bulk materials to use to hone your skills without planning to actually make a finished product from them. This way, when you're working with more expensive materials, or during a severe time crunch, you'll be more relaxed, you'll do better work, and you won't make as many mistakes.

TAKE CARE OF YOUR BODY
Crafting often requires fine, repetitive motions that can lead to painful joints, tendons, and muscles. Stretch deeply and often, especially after you've finished a lengthy work session. Support your body if need be, maybe with a pillow under your elbow or a special ergonomic sling or brace. Massage your muscles once you're done, and, most importantly, if you're starting to hurt,

stop. That pain isn't going to get better if you try to power through, so take a break, assess why you're hurting, rest, and adjust your technique.

THERE WILL BE MUD (AND DIRT, AND DUST, AND ALL SORTS OF FILTH)

Making things means making a mess. Keep your workspace clear and ventilated if you're making anything that involves chemical compounds or ground-up materials, as that stuff can give you all kinds of nasty conditions such as being dead. Wear a mask, open some windows and doors, and sweep up once you're done.

PLAN FOR TRANSPORTATION

Okay, now that you've put the finishing touches on your beautiful, custom bunk-bed shaped like Optimus Prime (the Generation 1 Peterbilt cab-over-engine Optimus, not that plebian Bayformer) and you've got someone willing to purchase it, you've run into a new problem—how to get it from Point Assembled to Point Buyer. If you make your sales through conventions, transportation is a little easier, as you won't have to worry about packing it for a shipping service. Otherwise, you'll need things like bubble wrap, packing paper, strong cardboard boxes and crates, and those little foam peanut thingies. When pricing your items online, include a shipping price that errs on the side of overestimating, as it's likely that you're going to underestimate how expensive shipping and materials are until you've been at this for a while.*

FOLLOW TRENDS . . .

Keep an eye on different trends in geekdom and build accordingly. If you like a meme that's sweeping the Internet, swoop in and build something based on that meme to drive up your potential traffic and SEO.†

---

* For more information on pricing your work, check out chapter eight of this very book (page 173)!
† That said, you should also use some grown-ass discretion when jumping on the meme bandwagons. Some memes perpetuate harmful stereotypes and ideas, or, in the case of the Tide Pod memes, which encouraged people to eat detergent, are flat-out dangerous.

. . . AND FOLLOW YOUR HEART

Craft things that excite you! If you're starting a build that requires eighty hours of work to complete, it won't feel as much like work if your end result is something you'd be proud to have yourself. Mix it up once in a while by crafting something outside of your wheelhouse.

RESEARCH!

Go beyond surface knowledge and do some research on the specifics of what you're making. Find other people who are doing what you're doing and absorb their advice, ask them questions, and learn from their mistakes and wisdom.

WORDS FROM WORKING NERDS

Bill Doran, who, along with his wife Brittany, runs Punished Props, which produces props, prop-making videos, tutorials, and books, like the Foamsmith trilogy*

I started doing prop-making as a hobby back in 2009, just for fun. Over a couple of years, I built up my skill set and reputation online before taking the plunge and making my hobby full-time in 2012. My wife and I have been running our business full-time for five years now, from the basement in our house. We're trying to figure out that "work/life balance" thing we've heard so much about; it's tough when the shop and office are a short flight of stairs away.

What's your daily schedule like?

Usually after breakfast we'll jump right into the shop to get to work on whatever project needs attention that day. I do a lot of video production, so sometimes that means video editing, but I also get plenty of time in the shop building props and costumes. That goes on till lunch, then after lunch it's back into the shop till dinner. If there's more to be done, we'll work after dinner, and lately we've been trying to get more downtime in the evenings. This cycle continues all seven days of the week. Some days are a little different, when we try to live-stream our process to our fans. In general, we spend as many hours a day as we can in building things and making content.

---

* Which is about prop-making, not a fantasy hero who crafts foam into weapons to save the land from a dark emperor.

What was your first paid, professionally nerdy project?

My brother commissioned me to build the Season 1 Colonial Pistol from the newer *Battlestar Galactica* TV show. He and his wife dressed up as Apollo and Starbuck for Halloween, and I made their sidearms.

Who or what are your inspirations?

There are a dozen or so other prop and costume makers who push me to be a better craftsman. Those include, but are not limited to: Harrison Krix, Svetlana and Benni Quindt, Zander Brandt, Steven K Smith, and Evil Ted Smith. These are makers of extraordinary skill who go well out of their way to share their processes with the community.

There is also a small handful of professional content creators whom I look up to. People like Tested (Adam Savage, Norman Chan, Frank Ippolito), Marc and Nicole Spagnuolo (The Wood Whisperer), Brian Brushwood (Scam School/The Modern Rogue), Bob Clagett (I Like to Make Stuff), and a couple more who really push me to be a better maker, content creator, and professional.

What should newcomers know?

The first couple of years are going to be rough. Don't count on making any money. What you should do is focus on honing your craft while making plenty of content (blog, video, podcast, etc.) to get your name out there. This content will help you draw income from as many sources as possible. If your only source of income is finished costumes for commissioned clients, then, while you're building it, you aren't making any money. The payday doesn't come until well after it's finished. Project durations differ wildly, based on the size and complexity of the build. A simple costume could take a few days, while a more complex outfit might take several months. That feast/famine roller coaster is absolutely soul-sucking.

Figure out other ways to make some income while you're working on longer-term projects. We make additional income from our YouTube ad revenue, Amazon affiliate links, and Patreon on top of what we might be paid for a sponsored or commissioned project. As far as our video content is concerned, we get at least one build tutorial video out per week (sometimes two or three). If the actual build takes longer than a week, the video can be split up into multiple parts and published over a several-week period. We also sell our instructional books on our website and Amazon.

It's taken us a few years to get the hang of it, but nowadays our revenue is much more consistent.

THE NEXT STEP: CRAFTING

Making a nerdy living is, among other things, a business. It may seem an ugly word to some of us beautiful creatives who don't want to think about base things such as profit margins and who instead simply want to *create*. But unless you're established/rich/lucky enough to have someone else take care of that for you, you're going to need to think like a businessperson sometimes.

MAKE YOUR OWN PRODUCT AND FIND THE DEMAND

Across Etsy and other crafted-item markets, there are people using taxidermy to create dioramas of mice in fanciful situations, and they're making *bank*. Weird? Maybe. Profitable? Hell yeah. Fifteen years ago, subscription boxes weren't really a thing, and yet for a while there you couldn't click through two pages online without tripping over an ad for someone's highly specialized subscription box full of shaving gear, healthful snacks, or Steve Urkel-themed fetish wear.

The Internet is a place with nigh-infinite room for niches; all you have to do is carve out the right niche and make it inviting to other like-minded people. Make something you're interested in, something you know people will want, and go online to find the demand for it.

IT'S BUSINESS TIME: HOW BIG IS YOUR CREW?

When your crafting business is composed entirely of you, there's a certain amount of freedom to be enjoyed. If you're a perfectionist, you can trust that everything's going to be done your way. If you're behind schedule, you don't have to worry about someone else breathing down your neck to get it done. If you enjoy peace and quiet, well, you'll find plenty of that, because you're on your own.

That said, human beings are a communal species for a reason—it's hard as hell getting stuff accomplished when you can only rely on yourself. Having a small team hits a nice sweet spot between having to do everything yourself and becoming so corporate that you don't get to do the stuff you like anymore, because you're too busy doing other important stuff.

Eventually, ideally, you will expand to the point of having employees, not just your buddies, working for you. At that point, the things you'll need to worry about will be keeping the business going smoothly so the folks whose mortgage payments depend on you will still have roofs over their heads while also not losing touch with the things that drew you to your business in the first place.

WORDS FROM WORKING NERDS

Tony Kim, CEO of the Hero Within clothing line, "a fashion brand that blends sophisticated style with pop culture"[23]

[Hero Within] grew as a progression of cosplay. In 2013 and '14, I would take the Comic-Con swag bags and convert them into costumes. I had a blazer one year and a jacket another, and it got a great response from Warner Bros. So working on a third year, myself and my design partner, we were about to do another jacket and I was like "I wonder if, instead of just doing another costume, we could take this idea and turn it into something more legitimate."

So instead of going to do a third year of cosplay, I did something that could turn into a ready-to-wear piece, which was a prototype of a Superman blazer. It wasn't refined, but it was a conversation piece. I shared it on my blog, which is great because my trip to Comic-Con became a focus group, and I realized this was something people might actually respond to. So the following year we made the decision to start the company and really go for it. It went from cosplay to trying something out at a Comic-Con and has turned into a company since then.

People ask me all the time what it's like to be an entrepreneur. There's a lot of focus and emphasis on a great idea that's unique, that tells a story, but people fail to think about the need for a great, knowledgeable, experienced, passionate team. The focus has really been on gathering a great team together who can really take this product and bring it to life. Thankfully, I have an amazing team. I've got one guy who's got a lot of experience in manufacturing and production, another guy who's great at partnerships, another who's great at social media, another who's great at operations, and we've got some part-time helpers as well.

How would you describe your job and daily life?

I say it's eight days a week, twenty-five hours a day, burning the candle on all three ends. If it's something that excites you and it's something you can get behind, do it, but this isn't for the faint of heart. That said, it's so *rewarding*. Nothing's better than getting an e-mail or phone call or seeing someone in person who has been looking for a Batman blazer their whole life, and they get into their own story with Hero Within, and they get into their own journey. I wouldn't trade it for the world. It's been an exciting ride.

How long does it take for a design to go from idea to finished product?

Normally from pencil-on-paper to actually delivering an entire stock of inventory, that's about six months, and that's being pretty aggressive. It takes a couple of months to do the design and research the iteration process. The first month is designing and the second month is sampling. It's one thing to make a product that looks cool, and it's another to make that same thing a thousand times over. Anyone can make a costume piece that looks awesome, but then it has to be manufactured in a timely and affordable way, so that all happens in the second month, and then it takes about three to four months to produce and deliver.

What would you say the challenges are of creating nerdy products?

Any company based on inventory is always challenging because it's a lot of manufacturing and fulfillment and warehousing and shipping and whatnot, so there's a ton of challenges along every step of the way.

As far as real "emotional work" challenges, recently we launched our Wonder Woman jacket, and it was really fascinating to see the spectrum of responses we got. We got men who were resistant to it, who felt like it was effeminate or emasculating and gave homophobic responses. What was interesting was how lots of fans embraced it and defended it by supporting it and buying/wearing it and posting about it. My vision the whole time has been that I don't want to make clothes that everyone's seen before. I want to make something new but also provoke thought and push the conversation forward. I love the fact that we'll be at a show and a couple will walk up. The guy will be like, "I don't know if I should wear Wonder Woman." And the girl will say, "I've been wearing Batman and Superman for years. How come you can't wear Wonder Woman?" And this encourages the guys to think about things in a new way.

What tips would you give to newcomers?

Don't do it! (laughs) If there's an easier way, go for it.

It's a roller coaster ride. What tipped me over the edge to do this was that I had a dream to do this, and then my life kind of kicked in, so this was something I had to develop over nights and weekends. And there was a point where I thought if I was ever going to do this, I had to throw myself into it, even though it was a risk when I had a pretty safe, pretty stable life. As luck would have it, in 2016 I lost my job, so I found myself in this place where I was like "Okay this is it; it's now or never." So I jumped in with both feet on this crazy roller coaster ride and spent all of 2016 waking up every day thinking "This is never going to work." I had that torturous thought every day of that year, and somehow it worked! Now I'm only thinking it every other day.

CONVENTIONS: BEHIND THE TABLE LIES A LAND OF WONDER AND HARD PLASTIC SEATS

If you want a career that's nerdy, you're probably going to be spending a lot of time at fan conventions. Shows such as San Diego Comic-Con, Wizard World, Dragon Con, and Golden Girls-A-Palooza are great ways for creators to connect with the people who enjoy their work. Though fan conventions may seem like impenetrable beasts for those who have never attended one, they're not nearly as scary as you've been led to believe. With a little knowledge and experience, you should have no problem getting out there to make money and meet people.

SUPER-ELITE SECRET ULTIMATE TIPS FOR BIG-TIME ULTRA SUCCESS AT BEING A CONVENTION EXHIBITOR

Plan your costs ahead of time. Hotels, parking passes, and the like cost cash. Find people to split the price with, and you'll breathe much easier.

Bring your own table cover. Convention tables don't always come with quality covers (or covers at all), so if you want your booth to look presentable, with room to hang signage, bring your own cover.

Get a banner. A banner should be colorful, retractable, and tall enough to be seen without being unmanageable. As a frequent con-goer, I can always spot the professionals versus the newbies, amateurs, and goobers wasting their money—the pros bring banners, backdrops, and fancy things for their booths. The newbies have signs they printed out using Microsoft Notepad, with their names written in ten-point type. Occasionally you'll get someone legit who lets their booth stay buck-naked with no decorations; these folks generate far less business than the people who look professional, inviting, and like they enjoy being there.

Be attentive to pre-show details. Pay promptly so you don't lose your spot, pay close attention to deadlines, and reach out to the people running the show if you need clarification.

Work up a good pitch. You will only have a handful of seconds to get the interest of those passing by your table. Think up some clever, friendly ways of greeting people to intrigue them into stopping by and maybe making a purchase. Try many different greetings to see which ones work best.

Learn how to chat with people. It's really highly recommended you have two people at your booth so that, when one of you gets locked into conversation, the other can still keep customers moving. Talking to people at cons is about connecting; find a way to connect what they're saying to what your message is . . . unless they're being a creep, in which case send 'em packing.

Learn who will or won't be interested in talking. People who are more likely to stop and buy something are those people who are responsive and chatty, people who are looking at your booth from three or fewer feet away, and people actively perusing your wares. People you're not likely to get to stop and buy something are folks on their phones, people glancing casually at your booth while walking quickly, people looking at your booth from more than three feet away, and elves.

Bring some stands. Book stands, print stands, Jojo's Bizarre Adventure Stands . . . If it'll help your merch stand out, bring it.

Find the food. Food is a serious limiting factor at a lot of conventions. If you go to the same shows year after year, you'll learn where the good eateries are. For shows you've never been to, or shows set in weird towns where there's nowhere good to freaking eat, plan ahead. Bring food with you—full meals if possible. Also, know that hotel breakfast buffet is a godly bonus at a convention; a nice big breakfast can make it easier to power through a long day that will later offer nothing but off-brand Mountain Dew and off-*off*-brand Twinkies that taste of leather. If you don't have good food options or a convention buddy to go grab food while you work the booth, you'll need to eat the best you can when the opportunity presents itself.

Learn about each convention. Talk to other people who regularly work booths at shows to see what their experiences have been.

Keep your stuff charged. Plugging in at night should be among your top priorities, and snagging a portable charger is a good idea.

Stay off your phone and out of your work. You're at the convention to sell your wonderful products and have a go at making a nerdy living, so stay the hell off your phone! Force yourself to look up and chat with people or you're never going to make any sales.

Plan and practice your answers. This varies a bit depending on what exactly you're selling at a con. For many occupations, you're going to get the same questions repeatedly. "What's this book about?" "Why'd you decide to make this?" "How did you get live Ewoks through customs?" Figure out smooth stock answers to the questions you want to answer, and evasive answering-without-really-answering statements for the questions you don't want to answer.

Get a good signature that's not the same one you use for legal documents. You don't want to sign an autograph the same way you sign important legal documents unless you really want to find yourself footing the bill for a wily identity thief's good time.

Bring extra writing utensils and extra cash to make change. Pens and markers aren't always reliable, and sometimes people will use that old-school currency called "cash" and will need you to make change.

Bring hand sanitizer. Convention Crud: the creeping illness that seems to make its way around every convention and infect attendees after they've gone home. Keeping a few bottles of hand sanitizer tucked discreetly away to use after handshakes will help keep the Con Crud down to a minimum.

Learn what each convention day is like. Most fan conventions run for three days—Friday, Saturday, and Sunday. Fridays are slower days for business, as the convention attendees are all mentally mapping out the booths and their wallets to see how much they want to spend. Saturdays are the big day, as the attendance is highest and most con-goers have figured out how much they're willing to spend. Sundays are a bit of a mystery day; at some shows, Sundays are walking dead with sparse attendance. Other shows will have a steady crowd on Sunday. Others still will have focused programming or discount deals for Sundays that will bring in particular types of crowds like, say, free admission for kids on Sundays.*

Pay attention to the particulars of each convention. Shows run by a blanket company, like Wizard World, have a (mostly) uniform way of doing things. Even so, most places are going to do things a little differently, meaning you'll need to pay attention to the con agreement when you sign up. What hours do they expect you to be there? What are the rules for sales tax? Will you have access to an electrical outlet at your booth? Will there be bright lights and

---

* Shows with free passes for kids are generally not good for your sales, as they attract big families looking for something cheap to do, not people who are looking to spend money.

loud sounds nearby to distract people away from your clever and welcoming sales pitch?

Have a way to make purchases with a credit card. Whether it's through an app, a phone add-on, or an old-fashioned credit card machine, don't miss out on those sweet, sweet card sales. People are a lot looser with intangible money than cash.

Use the hotel workout room, whatever it may be. Conventions are tiring experiences, despite the fact that working at one often involves a lot of sitting throughout the day. At night, even though you'll probably be tired, try to hop into the workout room for a quick bit of exercise. You'll sleep better, and your long-term health will thank you for it.

Make yourself valuable so you can sell your stuff for free. If you know how to put together great panels, you can net your party valuable convention passes and table space at no cost.

Don't be afraid to discount. If you've got customers who are on the fence about a purchase, offer them a discount or a special deal. You may not want to advertise said special deal up-front, though, so you can exercise it as a special weapon rather than the standard sales protocol.

Figure out what to sell, how to arrange your materials, etc. I've been at conventions where people passed my books by for hours only to have the floodgates of sales open up when I rearranged the way the books are spread out. Pay attention to your layouts and the amount of sales you're getting. Rearrange your goods once in a while if things are slow.

Know your rights as an exhibitor. Most people working shows are nice, hardworking folks. Every once in a while, however, you'll get someone who doesn't mind screwing over their fellow nerds. Maybe they're spilling their merch onto your table a bit, maybe they swapped your sweet corner table for their less-than-ideal location and blamed it on the convention organizers, or maybe they're being loud assholes whose lack of social skills is driving away customers. Whatever the issue may be, be firm but polite in discussing it with them. If they won't be reasonable, report them to the convention organizers. The people running conventions are inclined toward keeping the peace and are usually quick to jump on rule-breakers and misery-makers.

Set boundaries with the public. Sometimes people will hang out in front of your booth to make a phone call and block it for a while, or set a drink down on your table, or let their sticky-handed kid paw at your fragile merchandise. Again, firmly and politely inform the offending party to knock it off.

Check out the show a bit while you're there. Even after you've been to dozens of fan conventions, you'll still find they're all a little different. Wander the floor to check out the wares, chat with people, and give your body a break from sitting still all day.

No matter what you're building, few things are as satisfying as completing a finished product. For some of you, though, the thought of making things may sound enticing but you want to make something a little different. Something communal, something interactive, something bound by rules and dice and computer programming. If that's the case, perhaps you should consider entering the magical, mysterious world of game design.

CHAPTER FIVE

GAMING

We all play games,* and yet so few among us understand what makes a good game. This chapter will dive into the nitty-gritty of crafting a good gaming experience for players of any medium. In the days of yore, only a select few were allowed to ascend into the hallowed halls of the game-making industry. Now, with the advent of crowdfunding, all it takes to produce a game is the raw determination to get it made.

A (SELECTED) HISTORY OF HOME-BREWED GAMES: 8-BITS, TWENTY SIDES, AND SIXTY-FOUR COMMODORES

As a child, Gary Gygax would often dream up new types of games to play with his friends, creating rules and roles for the players to craft a unique experience in every session. As a teen, he was obsessed with fantasy, fiction, and board games. As an adult, his love of games expanded even as real-life worries encroached on all sides. Through determination and imagination, he and fellow game enthusiast Dave Arneson created a project with the working title The Fantasy Game, better known by its published name: Dungeons & Dragons.

Scott Cawthon has created video games since childhood; as an adult, he made several ill-received games that reviewers described as disturbing, citing the stiff animations and lifeless characters as having an accidentally eerie quality to them. Rather than let this discouragement stop him, Cawthon took it to heart and let it serve as the inspiration for his next game, a horror

---

* Especially that no-good man of yours, Susan. You need to dump him.

title about animatronics that came to life in a children's entertainment facility—and thus *Five Nights at Freddy's* was born. Since then, the franchise has boomed into countless other games, merchandise, and a book series, and it was optioned for a film adaptation within a year of its initial release.

Markus "Notch" Persson developed the game *Minecraft* while working a day job as a computer programmer. The game unofficially released in 2009, and as of 2018, Persson's estimated worth is $1.5 billion.*

Composer/game designer Toby Fox created the critically acclaimed *Undertale* using his experience creating a reprogrammed ROM hack of the game *EarthBound* and writing music for the multimedia webcomic *Homestuck*. Fox was in high school when creating his music and ROM hacks, and in college when he developed *Undertale*. *Undertale* released in 2015 when Fox, despite being just twenty-four years old, already had years of game-development experience.

Eric "ConcernedApe" Barone graduated from college with a computer-science degree. Unable to find a full-time job, he worked as an usher at a movie theater while dreaming up and developing his own game, *Stardew Valley*, a pleasantly addictive farming game which has gone on to sell millions of copies.

Matthew Inman created the webcomic/humor site The Oatmeal and leveraged that success to crowdfund a card game, Exploding Kittens, through Kickstarter. Exploding Kittens earned $8.7 million from its crowdfunding campaign alone.

A group of high school friends—Josh Dillon, Daniel Dranove, Eli Halpern, Ben Hantoot, David Munk, David Pinsof, Max Temkin, and Eliot Weinstein—worked together to crowdfund Cards Against Humanity, which earned over $15,000 through Kickstarter and has gone on to become the number-one selling game on Amazon, earning over $12 million in sales.[24]

While it would be great to be a Shigeru Miyamoto or Gary Gygax—a creative genius grandfathered in at the inception of a new gaming medium—you don't have to be Miyamoto or Gygax to become an accomplished game

---

* Based on his social media presence, he also seems to be a lonely jerk who says becoming rich and having all his dreams come true was a horrible thing.

designer. Cawthon, Persson, Fox, Barone, Inman, and countless others have all achieved great success by forging their own paths and reshaping the world of games through their singular determination. If you want to make the next great game, get to learning and get to *making*.

STARTING POINT: GAME DESIGN

Before you start playtesting, before you've picked out a catchy and thematically appropriate name for your game, before you've decided whether you're going to try your hand at developing video games, tabletop games, or something else altogether, there are a few tenets of game design all game designers need to understand.

PATTERNS OF REINFORCEMENT

Most behavioral psychologists hold firmly to the belief that living creatures operate based on patterns of reinforcement. We repeat behaviors that receive reinforcement (i.e., rewards), and we do not repeat behaviors for which we are punished. While punishment plays some part in game design, reinforcement is at the very core of the machine.

From a game-design standpoint, **schedules of reinforcement** are patterns that determine how frequently you reward your players. **Continuous schedules of reinforcement** reward players after every instance of a predetermined action, such as the set number of experience points you get for slaying a set type of monster. **Fixed-interval patterns of reinforcement** reward players after a specific amount of time has elapsed, like when a game requires an hour of in-game time to pass in order to craft a specific item. **Variable-interval patterns of reinforcement** reward players after variable amounts of time have passed; random rewards for periodically checking with an NPC (non-player character) or logging into a game, for example. **Fixed-ratio schedules of reinforcement** reward players after they take a fixed number of actions—e.g., quests that reward you for helping ten kobolds with their taxes or saving ten screaming babies from watching *Boss Baby* on repeat. **Variable-ratio schedules of reinforcement** reward players for variable numbers of actions taken, like when a player has the chance to get treasure at the end of a dungeon or a loot chest upon reaching an account milestone. Of the various schedules of reinforcement, variable-ratio is the most potent and the most addictive; it is the guiding principle around which Las Vegas and all gambling facilities build their businesses. Larger video games such as MMOs (massively multiplayer online games) will often combine numerous schedules of reinforcement to keep players multidirectionally engaged.

UNDERSTANDING THE TYPES OF PLAYERS

In order to figure out what sort of a schedule of reinforcement (or schedules of reinforcement) your game will operate on, you'll need to figure out what, exactly, the reinforcing element (or elements) of your game should be. Do you want to give players a triumphant feeling of accomplishment after completing a hard-won challenge? Do you want to grant a sense of status with powerful treasure for those who put in the hours to earn it? Is your game more about interacting with others than it is the raw game mechanics themselves? Whatever the case may be, you will need to examine the reinforcement patterns behind it to build the best game possible. If you can understand why players want to play your game, you will understand why they'll want to *keep* playing your game, and telling their friends about it, and buying add-ons and expansion packs.*

According to the Bartle taxonomy of player types,[25] game players fall into four multi-dimensional categories:

Achievers play for prestige. These players want recognition for their achievements; they crave the status that comes along with conquering a game and the knowledge that they have something to be admired. Elements such as rare in-game costumes, leaderboards for displaying high scores, and achievement points appeal to the achievers. Those who push their skills to the limit to conquer hard-earned single-player challenges such as toppling *Spelunky*'s super-secret final boss King Yama are achievers.

---

* Your more story-driven video games are far less about patterns of reinforcement than they are about creating an engaging narrative. *Undertale* didn't become a smash hit through its game mechanics alone; it became a hit, in large part, thanks to its memorable characters, evocative themes, and sharp writing. Chapter nine (page 193) will cover such storytelling elements in greater detail.

Socializers play games for the interaction with other players. These folks use a game as a means of hanging out; the actual game experience is secondary to their enjoyment of the engagement they get from other people. The folks you see standing around in *Destiny*'s social hubs break-dancing are, among other things, socializers.

Explorers play games for the immersive experience. They enjoy the feeling of wandering, scouring the nooks and crannies of a game, stumbling across secrets and Easter eggs, fully losing themselves in these virtual worlds. Those of us who've lost countless hours in the winter wonderland of *Skyrim* are explorers.

Killers play games for the competition. To put it succinctly, they want to show others they're better than them by defeating them. Competitive multiplayer games are of particular interest to killers, as it gives a platform through which they can show off their skills in the spirit of (hopefully) friendly competition. Those who play fighting games such as *Street Fighter* are killers.

Board games, by their very nature, have a heavy element of socialization to them, with an emphasis on Killer elements and a secondary emphasis on Achiever elements. Video games, on the other hand, are more complex and free-form. While creating your game, consider the type of games *you* enjoy, and what you enjoy about them, to acquire deeper insight into the types of gamers you want your game to appeal to.

Note that few players are going to be a singular type of player at all times. Sometimes you might be in the mood to smash some heads in *Tekken*. Sometimes you might be in the mood to make some friends in *Animal Crossing*. Sometimes you feel like swinging around on a grappling hook in *Just Cause*. The trick as a game designer is to find a way to satisfy the players drawn to your type of game while also to entice new players who might not ordinarily play your game.

CHOOSING A STYLE OF GAME

As with any type of creative expression, knowing the genre you wish to express yourself in is less about constraining your creativity and more about understanding the type of reaction you wish to elicit from your audience. With games, we have a massive diversity of genres because there's such a diversity of potential audience reactions and interactions.

Action games, which are about giving players fast-paced interactions and pulse-pounding excitement, usually by challenging their reflexes and manual dexterity.

- ◆ **Video game examples**: *Uncharted, Devil May Cry, Bayonetta*
- ◆ **Tabletop game examples**: Jenga, Dungeon Fighter, Terror in Meeple City

Adventure games, which are about providing players with a thrilling world to explore.

- ◆ **Video game examples**: *Metal Gear Solid, Monkey Island, Thimbleweed Park, Metroid, The Legend of Zelda, Assassin's Creed*
- ◆ **Tabletop game examples**: Betrayal at House on the Hill, Hero Quest

Role-playing games, which are about immersing players in the role of a character, emphasize story and narrative over minute-to-minute action.

- ◆ **Video game examples**: *Persona, Mass Effect, Fallout, Divinity*
- ◆ **Tabletop game examples**: Dungeons & Dragons, Vampire: The Masquerade, Shadowrun, Fiasco

Simulation games, which are about providing a fun, gamified version of some·aspect of reality.

- ◆ **Video game examples**: Pretty much any game with the word *simulator* in it, like *Flight Simulator, Farm Simulator,* or *Simulation Game Simulator*
- ◆ **Tabletop game examples**: Settlers of Catan, Alhambra

Puzzle games are about challenging the dexterity of the mind, and not the fingers, with carefully constructed enigmas to be solved.

- ◆ **Video game examples**: *Toki Tori, Portal, The Talos Principle, Rush*
- ◆ **Tabletop game examples**: jigsaw puzzles, Rubik's cubes, Sudoku

Strategy games are about mentally surpassing your opponents by thinking long-term.

- ◆ **Video game examples**: *Starcraft, Civilization, X-Com*
- ◆ **Tabletop game examples**: Warhammer, Ticket to Ride, Risk, Chess

Social/party games are about fostering interaction between players using the game world.

- ◆ **Video game examples**: *Mario Kart, Mario Party, Keep Talking and No One Explodes, You Don't Know Jack*
- ◆ **Tabletop game examples**: The Resistance, Werewolf, Cranium

As always, genre is a mutable concept open to interpretation and cross-pollination. *The Legend of Zelda* games have a lot of adventure to them, but they also have elements of action and puzzle-solving, too. Your game can be more than one thing, so long as you don't lose sight of the experience you want your players to have.

MAKING MODS AND HOME-BREWED RULES: GETTING YOUR FEET WET IN THE BIG-ASS POOL OF GAME DESIGN

Most game designers don't start their careers by jumping into making a professional game on a triple-A budget on day one; instead, they make games at home or modify their favorite games to better understand them.

The team behind the retro-fueled delight *Sonic Mania* got its start making mods of old *Sonic the Hedgehog* games, tweaking the graphics, gameplay, and levels into something new. Sega got wind of these talented cats and let them use what they'd learned making mods to work on ports of the *Sonic* games they'd been modding for years. From there, the team then got the chance to create their own *Sonic* game with *Sonic Mania*.

Warcraft 3 player Icefrog famously created and polished a *Warcraft 3* mod called *Defense of the Ancients*. This mod became so popular it grew into its own licensed game and became the forefather for an all-new type of game, the MOBA (multiplayer online battle arena). Today *Dota 2*, *League of Legends*, and *Heroes of the Storm* are among the most popular games on the planet, with hundreds of millions of players and an unfathomable number of hours sunken into them.

Countless tabletop game designers grew up playing their own home-brewed versions of games, creating house rules they felt sanded off some of the rougher edges of their favorite games. If you've ever modified Monopoly by either making custom deals with other players or by putting money from tax fines into the Free Parking square, you've played by house rules.

Game designer Kim Pittman grew up home-brewing and DM'ing (dungeonmastering) Dungeons & Dragons with her brother, something she states gave her invaluable experience when it came to both designing games and playing them.[26] Dungeons & Dragons's free-form nature encourages creativity, which makes for both better players and better game-makers. Making mods and home-brewing rules and game types is a natural way for young designers to get their feet wet in the deep ocean of game design.

PLAYING GAMES PROFESSIONALLY

Now, some of you have read the basic principles of game design and are drooling to get more in-depth about the philosophies and psychology behind the games we play. Others of you have felt less interested in the behind-the-scenes stuff and are more interested in diving in and playing games that are already made. If that's the case, you may want to try your hand at playing games professionally or streaming games as entertainment.

Today there are thousands of professional gamers whose livelihood is tied directly to their skills with a controller. These pros win tournaments, earn sponsorships, have coaches, and get recruited to teams exactly like their more conventional sporting contemporaries. To be a professional gamer requires you to find a game (or games) you're passionate about— that you don't mind studying exhaustively, obsessively, and academically. You'll have to take training seriously and study to stay up to date on the latest technology and techniques.

To do this, you'll need to be both unsociable and sociable. The former because it takes an extraordinary amount of practice to get competitive at a game; the latter because you're going to play harder, and play longer, if you've got friends to play with. One of the reasons Venus and Serena Williams are such legendarily skilled tennis players is that the twin sisters have always had each other to train with. If you're constantly butting heads against opponents of similar skill, you'll constantly find improvement. If all you do is stomp the poots out of your real-life friends who don't really know how to play your game, you're not going to get any better. The online environment makes it easier than ever to find nice folks to play with. Scour chat channels and random matches for people with good skills and good attitudes.

Finally, if you'd rather just entertain people by streaming games, well, we covered that pretty thoroughly back in chapter two (page 31).

THE NEXT STEP: GAME DESIGN

What do we want? Satisfying games! When do we want them? Two weeks ago, we're seriously behind schedule, like, holy cow there's a lot of work that goes into making games.

To make the right games, you're going to need the right tools, such as:

A COMPUTER

Whether your games are digital or pen-and-paper, you're not likely to get very far without the processing and planning power of a computer.

PROGRAMS

There are countless computer programs you can use; ultimately, it depends on your skill, preference, and the type of game you're making.

Twine® is a very straightforward, easy-to-understand program that eschews complex programming language to give creators a good starting point for building their games. There are limited options as far as what you can make without doing some serious programming of your own, and action-y games are completely out of the question, but if you're looking to make something slower and textier, you'll be sure to have a nice, clean, functional product once you're finished.

Stencyl's interface is a bit more complex than Twine's; with that complexity comes an increased versatility of game design. Stencyl will allow you to easily export your games to smart phones and PCs alike.

If you want to make a retro RPG (role-playing game), RPG Maker® is a powerful program to let you do so. It's easy to import your own files, like music and art, and the game engine is powerful enough to let you add in your own systems to the code. Just make sure you (mostly) use original art and music instead of the generic placeholders that come with RPG Maker—RPG fans can spot them a mile away, and they're a huge turnoff.

Game Maker Studio is incredibly powerful, can make nearly anything you can imagine, and comes with a built-in tutorial. *Spelunky*, *Hyper Light Drifter*, and *Undertale* were all built using Game Maker Studio.

ART

Unless you're going to make a text adventure, you'll need some art. Adobe Photoshop and Adobe Illustrator® are commonly used, high-power programs that come with a variably high price. Free programs like Manga Studio® can fit the bill, depending on what you're looking for, but ultimately you should use whatever program you feel most comfortable with. I mean, for cryin' out loud, Toby Fox used Microsoft Paint to make the art for *Undertale*!

If you're a bit lacking on the artistic side, websites like Freesound.org and OpenGameArt.org provide quality audio/visual resources you can use without cost. I would recommend that if you don't know how to make music you consider paying someone to create a few tunes for your game. Just having a good title theme, game-over theme, and level complete/victory theme can go a long way toward giving your game a memorable, unique feel.

If you're making a board/tabletop game, you'll need boards, figurines, dice, etc. While playtesting in small groups, you can probably cobble together something from the dice and figurines you already own. As you progress, you'll want to ditch the placeholders to have something that better fits your game, which will require you to either learn to make such items yourself or to hire someone you can count on to deliver the art you need.

PLAYTESTERS

All right, #realtalk, being a video game playtester is not an especially fun job. You're not sitting around playing games all day, you're running a character into walls for nine hours to see if you can clip through them. As an indie game developer, your playtesters are most likely going to be your friends and family. Be nice to them, and listen when they tell you that something doesn't make sense or isn't fun.

Playtesting board games, on the other hand, will require a lot of work out of you to keep an eye on your players to see when they get bored and confused by the rules. It also means you're going to spend a lot of time playing your game with people or *trying* to get them to play it (come on, guys, we fixed the resource overflow problem, it'll be fun this time, I swear!).

BE REALISTIC, START SMALL, AND FIGHT TO KEEP THE FOCUS SMALL

When I was in junior high, a friend of mine was so inspired by *Ultima Online* that he said he too was going to make an MMO. His game was going to be even bigger than *Ultima Online*, with more world to explore, more skills to master, more monsters to fight, and more game systems to make it even gamier. We talked endlessly, excitedly about this game, but in the back of my mind I kept wondering where he would find the time to finish such a gargantuan project. The kind of scope he was talking about was insane, *especially* for a kid with next to no programming experience under his belt. He'd become Feature Creep* personified, and for all his dreaming he ended up with exactly nothing in the way of a playable game.

Meanwhile, I plugged away at RPG Maker 2003, the free game-making program that lets you build Super Nintendo–esque role-playing games. I planned modestly, kept the focus small, and tried to tell an intimate story with a limited cast of characters. As I went along, the game and its cast expanded beyond what I'd initially planned. Thankfully, since I'd planned ahead, I was able to finish my game—a short, not especially good, but very heartfelt RPG that clocks in at a hair over ten hours of playtime.

When designing your game, keep your focus small, as the game will inevitably expand. A massive, unfinished game is a pile of badly coded crap. A small, finished game, however, is a *finished game*.

GAMES CAN BE MORE THAN WAYS TO PASS THE TIME

With most games, I will watch the first handful of cutscenes to see if the writing quality in the game is worth my time. Far more often than not, I'll end up skipping most of the subsequent cutscenes because the writing is garbage, so who cares?

Far too few game designers are concerned with making a good story, instead satisfying themselves with being a platform through which big companies can entice customers into making repeat purchases. Games can be art; make yours a masterpiece.

---

* A gaming industry term for when the scope of a game continues expanding during development, slowing down development time and increasing cost.

KEEP YOUR PLAYERS FOCUSED

Few things feel crappier, as a DM, than crafting what you think is going to be an awesome encounter, only to look around and see unengaged players.

Anticipate what your players will think; keep them focused on whatever is most engaging. Listen to their feedback and incorporate it into your game.

LET YOUR PLAYERS SUCCEED

A game can be soul-crushingly hard but still fun to play so long as you give players a sense of success, even if the success is as small as "I made it three steps past that dragon that keeps killing me!" The *Dark Souls* series, famous for its tagline "Prepare to die," has a devoted fanbase thanks to providing a sense of satisfaction to players even when they inevitably die. A player succeeds if they're satisfied with a feeling of progress, not necessarily just when they beat a boss or conquer a level.

COUNT ON YOURSELF FIRST, COUNT ON YOURSELF LAST

Other people are notoriously unreliable.* They will often have good intentions and may get very excited at the prospect of working on a game. Ultimately, though, *you* are the most reliable person you have. Share the work when you can, make plenty of backups and contingency plans in case someone falls through or wigs out and runs off with your data, and go into your project with the knowledge that you are probably going to be doing the bulk of the work yourself.

STUDY GAMES

Read books and articles about game design. Think critically about the games you play, analyzing what works and doesn't work. Attend lectures (or watch virtual lectures). Like any creative field, making good games means you will need to put time and effort into figuring out what makes something good.

AVOID THE PLAGIARISM PLAGUE

Don't use other people's code without their permission in a game you're trying to make money from. That is—say it with me, class—*stealing*!

---

* Especially Susan's boyfriend, Steve. You can't count on that dude for *anything*.

THE POWER OF THE PEOPLE: CROWDFUNDING THE GAME YOU'VE ALWAYS WANTED TO MAKE

While the game industry is very much alive and well, things have changed. Crowdfunding has given freedom to game-makers in a way we've never seen before. Small studios like Yacht Club Games (*Shovel Knight*), famous developers such as Koji Igarashi (*Castlevania* producer, *Bloodstained: Ritual of the Night*) and Keiji Inafune (*Mega Man* producer, *Mighty No. 9*), and indie developers who have no previous major experience (Matthew Inman, Exploding Kittens) have all used crowdfunding to great success.

So how can you get your game successfully funded? The easiest way is to be independently wealthy already and pay for it yourself; barring that, you could also try being famous or owning the rights to make a sequel to an established property. Or, I guess if you want to do things the *hard* way by not already being rich and famous, there are a few ways to up the odds of successful crowdfunding.

1. **Make a polished proof-of-concept design.** Having a great idea won't get you money; you need to show your audience that you know how to translate that good idea into a palpable reality. In your crowdfunding video, show a placeholder version of your game in action. Hire a good artist (or con a friend) into creating good concept art to go along with your crowdfunding campaign to give potential backers an idea of what the finished concept is going to be.

2. **Perfect your crowdfunding video.** The term *elevator pitch* refers to the lightning-fast description you would use to pitch your book/movie/series idea to a producer or publisher if you should be so lucky as to get in an elevator with them. Your crowdfunding video is an elevator pitch, and the producers are the entire Internet. Make your video perfect and professional to show the world that you have the dream, the energy to get it accomplished, and the foresight to plan smartly; show that all you're lacking is the capital to get started.

3. **Reach out to gaming publications.** The Internet is littered with gaming blogs and sites. Contact their writers and editors about your campaign with a professional, yet entertaining, e-mail. Get them interested, and they'll get *their* readers interested.

4. **Be prepared to spend a lot of time managing things during your crowdfunding campaign.** Crowdfunding makes for a nerve-wracking month or two. You can't leave your campaign running without supervision; you'll need to check and manage it constantly. Crowdfunding campaigns are less "house cat" and more "newborn baby."

5. **Utilize social media.** As with all livings nerdy, make use of social media to advertise your game and crowdfunding campaign. If you've got any favors with people who have a big audience, call them in to get them to help pitch you. Also, connect with people. Follow the comments and interact with those who have questions or who are interested in your game. The Internet's not just a place for people to yell slurs at one another; sometimes it's a place where strangers can chat and have a nice time.

After all this, let me end this chapter with the warning that game-making can be a harsh, stressful field. The video game industry is infamous for the ludicrous amount of unpaid extra hours its employees are expected to work when products are behind schedule (which they always are) or close to shipping. Tabletop games, though their popularity has certainly increased in recent years, are still a somewhat more niche market and therefore harder to break into and stay successful in. If game-making is your passion, however, no amount of crunch time or niche-ness can stop you.

For some of you, maybe game-making isn't your true passion. In fact, just reading this chapter has made you realize that you, against all odds, like your current job. With that in mind, let's step back from focusing on breaking into new jobs and instead discuss ways of making your current gig a little more fun and a lot more nerdy.

CHAPTER SIX

BRINGING UNCONVENTIONAL NERDINESS TO CONVENTIONAL CAREERS

Playing video games for a living, web-streaming live shows, and cosplaying as fictional characters are as nontraditional as careers get. For some folks, however, their passion lies in older types of careers, yet they still also crave a way to infuse their love of nerdiness into these non-nerdy jobs. Great! If you've got a job you love, no matter what it is, enjoy it!*

The most obvious traditional career to infuse nerdiness into would be academia. Academics are the original nerds—analyzing and obsessing over their fields of study to gain exceptional levels of understanding. Dr. Neil deGrasse Tyson has a profound love of the cosmos, and by blending pop culture with science he acts as a scientific ambassador to get people interested.

Danica McKellar, in addition to her many acting credits that include *The Wonder Years, Young Justice,* and *Project MC2,* has used her considerable mathematical skills to author a book series that breaks difficult mathematical concepts down in math newbie–friendly ways. McKellar's books are for everyone who could use a little extra help with math, but they also have an extra emphasis on encouraging girls to understand and appreciate the wacky world of numbers, as girls are all too often discouraged from STEM fields.

Outside the academic sector, there are still plenty of options to meld nerdiness with business; all it takes is for you to put your big mind to it.

---

* I mean, maybe with a few exceptions, like if you're a professional torturer or something.

WORDS FROM WORKING NERDS

Psychologist **Dr. Travis Langley** is a lifelong nerd (and my dad) who melded his love of psychology with his love of popular culture in his Psychology of Fiction series, with entries such as *The Walking Dead Psychology: Psych of the Living Dead, Star Wars Psychology: the Dark Side of the Mind,* and *Batman and Psychology: A Dark and Stormy Knight.*

Since third grade, I knew I had to write. Whether I was going to become a journalist or novelist or comic book writer, I would become an author. And I was always fascinated with storytelling—both fiction and nonfiction. We learn through stories. We share human experience through stories. I wanted to write, and I wanted to understand people. In fourth grade I checked a psychology book out from the library. I didn't understand much of it, but, by gosh, I tried.

By the time I became a professor, I didn't want to write a textbook. I wanted to tell stories. I used to think of the academic side of my life and the author side as two separate things. Once these two tracks merged and became the same thing, it was the truest to myself I'd ever felt. There was no longer this other part of me that I didn't share at the office. I'm the professor who wrote a book on the psychology of Batman. That's still what I'm best known for, and that feels pretty darn good. It's a long way from being a kid who loved heroic fiction, especially comic books, and had no peers to discuss that with.

What inspired you to incorporate nerdy elements into your work?

First, a communication professor at my university named Randy Duncan paved the way, uniting the scholarly and the nerdy by teaching a course on comics as communication, working on a textbook about that, advising a comic book-lovers club, getting our library to build an impressive graphic novel collection, and bringing creators to speak at our university as guests. When he took a group of our students to visit the offices of DC Comics, my son Nicholas and I went along with them.

A lot of things came together one summer ten years ago. I taught a course on psychology in literature for the first time. Among the many readings, I assigned one comic book issue and one graphic novel. Each student had to choose one fictional character to analyze in many different ways—Hamlet, Captain Ahab, Moll Flanders—and to show them how to do the tasks, I did them myself with Batman as the example. That same summer, I attended the Comics Arts Conference, a scholarly set of panels at San Diego Comic-Con, because I wanted to see Nicholas on a panel about student research. Something I wrote for that same conference later became a journal article and eventually laid the foundation for a book, *Captain America vs. Iron Man*. On my way to Comic-Con, I read a book by Danny Fingeroth, *Superman on the Couch*, which made me think "I want to write this kind of book." At Comic-Con, I saw people animated, invigorated by the celebration of interests that make them feel ostracized [at] other places in their lives. I met comics scholars. I knew I needed to write a journal article about Batman. Within a year, I knew I needed to write a book about Batman.

Who or what are your inspirations?

My sons. I got involved in comic cons to help them find and follow their passions, and that changed the course of mine. Their mom—my wife, Rebecca—gives me insight and makes me laugh. Find inspiration around you, and be inspired for their sakes.

Randy Duncan and Danny Fingeroth [are inspirations], for reasons I mentioned. Michael Uslan developed the first course on comics as folklore at an accredited university and went on to become the first doctor of comic books and the executive producer of the Batman movies. Gail Simone was a hairdresser whose passion led her to become one of the most successful comic book writers today. It's been an honor to get to know them all.

Psychologist William Moulton Marston inspires me because he managed to make contributions in the field of psychology and to create Wonder Woman, and his granddaughter Christie inspires me with everything she has built to help people from around the world connect and share their love of that character.

Passion transcends topics. One of the wonderful things about a fan convention is that you and someone you just met might share the same interests, or you might have completely different interests but still understand each other's passion.

The fervor of people who build and craft fascinates me. So many devoted cosplayers invest time and love bringing costume creations to life. People who work in special effects like Eliot Sirota and Fon Davis, a propmaker such as Bill Doran, the furniture maker who reupholstered my grandparents' chairs, and a lot of people you might be interviewing for this book—they're making things. Some make money at it. Even those who don't can live more fully for it. They earn *emotional wealth*. Money's just numbers.

These individuals do not settle for drudging along through this existence. Even if it doesn't always feel like it, they *live*.

What tips do you have for anyone looking to incorporate their nerdy loves into their less-nerdy jobs?

Find your people. Find your passion. Find what you love in life and celebrate it. Maybe you can't be open about it in one setting, like your place of work, but find somewhere else where you can be. If you can be open at work, maybe by doing something as simple as hanging a *Star Wars* calendar on your wall, you'll likely find that there are others around who'd love to talk about *Star Wars*, too. Because I'm open to the whole world about my interests, there are faculty and staff members I cross paths with who strike up conversations with me about *The Walking Dead*, *Star Trek*, and comic book movies. Sometimes you have to conceal it at work because you're not working around people who will understand, but the sooner you can treat it as no big deal, the truer to yourself you'll feel.

BE CREATIVE ANYWHERE, NO MATTER HOW SMALL
THAT PLACE MAY BE

At a butcher's shop, shape a pile of beef into the Death Star to let people know you're running a special for Alderaan Memorial Day.* If you work anywhere with a dry-erase board, go nuts with the nerdy fan art. It'll give you a chance to flex your artistic skills, and it may get some attention online.

INFLUENCE PRODUCT SELECTION

If you work where you have a say in what gets stocked, try to stock some products that align with your interests. If you work in a bookstore, work on expanding the selection of manga and graphic novels. If you work at a clothing store, see if you can get in a few T-shirts with some robots or X-people on 'em.

MAKE A NERDY VERSION OF NON-NERDY ENTERTAINMENT
AND NON-NERDY BUSINESSES

Thanks to nerd culture's spread into mainstream culture, we've seen a rise in people finding new and interesting ways to express their nerdiness. There are burlesque shows such as D20 Burlesque and Nerd Girl Burlesque. There are also bands like Okilly Dokilly, a Ned Flanders–themed metal band; the Klingon death-metal band, Stovakor; the McDonald's-themed Black Sabbath group, Mac Sabbath; and countless other musical groups who build their style and sound from science, gaming, and popular culture.

As seen in the film *Trekkies*, dentist Dennis Bourguignon and his wife Shelly modified their dental practice to give it a *Star Trek* flair. This satisfied both their love of science fiction and their desire to portray dentists as "good-doers." There's the *Doctor Who*–themed Pandorica in Beacon, New York; Los Angeles's Library Bar, which mixes heavy drinking with heavy reading; New York City's haunted house–esque Jekyll & Hyde Club; and many other such entertaining eateries and establishments.

Nerdy businesses *are* a little harder to get off the ground, given that they're focusing on a more niche experience, but the only way to truly fail at doing something is to never try in the first place.

---

* Although using a Death Star to commemorate the planet it blew up is pretty messed up, dude.

START A CLUB

Your office may not be a nerdy place, but if your workplace is large enough, there could be a few other folks who would like to talk about live-streaming games, Dungeons & Dragons, which of the crystal gems on *Steven Universe* is the best dancer,* etc. Be the brave soul to put yourself out there with a pamphlet and a reserved room to transform the occasional lunchtime into a moment to recharge your nerdy batteries with like-minded peeps. At my alma mater, Henderson State University, the pop culture–themed club Legion of Nerds quickly became the largest organization on campus after its inception— after I'd already graduated, alas.

UNCOVER A VAST CONSPIRACY

It takes some seriously nerdy work to find the various connections between seemingly random people, places, and events, and then to cover several walls in newspaper clippings, online articles, and photographs tied together with red string. Your work may suffer; that doesn't matter anymore, not now that you've realized just how *deep* this whole thing goes.

FOSTER A HATRED FOR YOUR JOB SO INTENSE THAT YOU LOSE TOUCH WITH SANITY COMPLETELY

This job sucks. You should instead go to work as your Dungeons & Dragons character. Summon a big hairy demon for some laughs. Bark at the moon. Speak only in R'lyehian. Dehumanize yourself and face to bloodshed.

RETURN FROM THE BRINK OF MADNESS AND FIND A NEW JOB IF YOU DON'T LIKE YOUR CURRENT GIG

Orrrrr maybe take a breather, calm down, and figure some things out instead of going full-on banaynays.

Developmental psychologist Erik Erikson's research led him to theorize that human beings go through specific psychosocial crises during specific times of life. As teens and young adults, we're in a stage of *identity vs. role*

---

* The correct answer, of course, is Captain Picard.

confusion, trying to ascertain who we are, where we fit in, what we want to be, and all those other questions that keep us up at night. By exploring multiple venues of identity while we're young, Erikson believed we could come to a healthy conclusion about the self. So, basically, explore your options!

Erikson posited that, as we reach middle age, humans go through *generativity vs. stagnation*. During this stage, we take stock of our lives to determine whether we feel we're being *generative*—building things that give us a sense of purpose—or *stagnant*—stuck in a place we don't want to be. Now whether middle-aged or not, stagnation isn't something anyone wants to experience; we want to know our lives have *meaning*, that we're doing more than toiling away every day to keep our bodies functioning.

Don't just do what's expected of you. Change majors and careers if need be. Don't settle for a career path if you find you don't really like it once you've started on it. You may go through school to get a degree only to realize once you're holding your diploma that you don't really want to *do* anything involving that degree. Mythbuster Jamie Hyneman holds a degree in Russian linguistics. I don't think Mr. Hyneman spoke a lick of Russian on the show, but he's doing pretty well for himself in the fields of engineering and entertainment.

As long as you learn from what you've done, you will never waste your time. Thanks to my degrees in psychology, I'm able to infuse a lot of psych-related wisdom into my writing (hence the red-hot Erikson knowledge I dropped earlier). I don't technically need a background in psych to write books, but it's helped shape me into who I am, so in a way, it's exactly the background I need.

Ultimately, you need to search yourself. Find the career you want and start doing whatever it is that will take you toward that career. That's what this whole book is about, isn't it?

"Hmm . . ." you say, "these careers sound nice, but I live in an area where the job selection is limited and also garbage. I want to do something vivacious, something that lets me combine my extensive, eclectic knowledge base with my propensity for boisterous performing and active listening. Maybe something where I can call in my friends to do easy off-camera work."

If these are the sorts of things you find yourself contemplating, friend, then you might just be cut out for the wild world of podcasting.

WORDS FROM WORKING NERDS

Dr. Janina Scarlet, psychologist, author, and full-time geek, is most known for superhero therapy, which incorporates pop culture into evidence-based or research-supported therapy to provide treatments for anxiety, depression, and post-traumatic stress disorder.

How did you get started incorporating popular culture into your therapeutic treatments?

I think I've known most of my life I wanted to become a psychologist. I didn't know exactly how or why, but I always wanted to help people. It wasn't until I started working with active-duty Marines that it became clear to me I really wanted to incorporate pop culture into therapy in this way. I've always been a fan of pop culture, and the X-Men were kind of my gateway into geekdom, but the way it started was during my postdoctoral training of working with active-duty Marines with PTSD (post-traumatic stress disorder). Many of them reported feeling ashamed for having developed PTSD. Many of them would say they wanted to be Superman and that they felt like failures. So in talking about Superman, we were able to find that he actually has a number of vulnerabilities [that don't] make him any less of a superhero, and we were able to use that as part of cognitive processing therapy. And I saw the benefits this work had. Later, I started doing a few more [therapies] with other types of pop culture and started incorporating more characters from things like Game of Thrones, *The Walking Dead*, Harry Potter, and Star Wars, and I've seen huge benefits from doing that.

What has surprised you most with Superhero Therapy?

I thought people might be thrown off by it or be uncomfortable. I've actually found that most psychologists and other therapists and patients seem to be really excited about it. Of course, it's not for everyone, but most people are really open to the idea of incorporating pop culture into therapy and using creativity in this way. People feel less alone and more connected. I've been very blessed and grateful to have such warm, positive feedback, and a lot of therapists are now attending my workshops and reporting huge benefits for their own patients.

What advice would you give to other people looking to incorporate their nerdy loves into their less-than-nerdy careers?

The best advice I can give is to go with your heart. If you are really interested in psychology, you can do that with your own tweaks and elements. I know people who are incorporating Dungeons & Dragons or Magic: The Gathering into therapy, and that's really successful, too. You could also incorporate other kinds of music or art. . . . I think there's no limit to what we can do. If you're a nerd, if there's something you're really passionate about, if you can tie it into your daily life, [then] I think not only will it be exciting for you but for other people as well, and it will really improve your quality of life. I think that when work is fun, that's when it's the best kind of reward someone can have.

Who are some people who have inspired you in your work?

Fiction- and writer-wise, Neil Gaiman and J. K. Rowling, because of the way their writing has touched so many lives and helped people on so many different levels. As a psychologist, I'm a big fan of Kristen Neff's work and Kelly McGonigal. I think those two women have taken their nerdy passions for research and combined it with something they're passionate about, like self-compassion and health psychology, and revolutionized the way we study psychology. I think all my role models are people who have found a way to follow their hearts and be creative in a way that not only helps them [but also] helps people around the world.

CHAPTER SEVEN

PODCASTING

T he spoken word is a form of entertainment stretching back to the start of human history, when the first cave person grunted wry observations about cave life to the amusement and enlightenment of his fellow crap-flingers. Today our desire for entertainment and wisdom remains the same, but the delivery system has changed.* Smartphones bring us unfettered access to the world of sound wherever we go, and with that freedom to listen comes the desire for something worth listening to.

THE HISTORY OF PODCASTS

In the early '00s, Adam Curry and Dave Winer—the same Dave Winer who helped create blogs—helped build rich site summary (RSS) feeds for audio-heavy content known as *audiologs*. This paved the way for podcasts.[27] Winer then worked with former *New York Times* reporter Christopher Lydon to expand his blog to include audiologs of his in-depth interviews with techno-logically minded and important people, creating what many argue to be the first podcast series.

For the next few years, podcasts were by cutting-edge people, for cutting-edge people. They weren't easy to get into the hands of the general public, partly due to technological limitations and partly because most people had never heard of podcasts before.

In 2005, iTunes added native support for podcasts, meaning that any-one with an Apple device could easily find a podcast and start listening. This

---

* For one thing, today's verbal exchanges end far less frequently in the flinging of feces.

marked a tectonic shift in the zeitgeist that is still quaking to this day, as the popularity of podcasts continues to grow.

Comedians were among the first to adopt the format to full effect. Ricky Gervais, Stephen Merchant, and their perpetually curmudgeonly friend Karl Pilkington, created *The Ricky Gervais Show* to international success. Chris Hardwick, frustrated with having to wait around hoping for acting and comedy work to present itself, started the *Nerdist* podcast in 2010 as a way of empowering himself to generate his own work. Today, *Nerdist* has become a multimedia empire known as Nerdist Industries. Mustachioed misanthrope Marc Maron's *WTF with Marc Maron* interviewed many guests over the years, though none as noteworthy as President Barack Obama. This interview was the first time a podcast had featured an American president as its guest, thus helping solidify the medium as an important means of communication.

Filmmaker-turned-B-filmmaker-and-podcaster Kevin Smith supported the medium of podcasting from almost the beginning of its existence. Smith's Smodcast network is home to dozens of different shows, several of which feature the enthusiastic tones of Smith himself. As someone who likes to sit around, get high, and make dirty jokes, Smith's brand of gentle vulgarity was perfect for podcasting's freely accessible format, netting him a massive army of followers and listeners.

As podcasts continue to increase in popularity, so too do the myriad ways in which people utilize them to tell stories, educate, and entertain. *This American Life, Serial, Stuff You Should Know, Welcome to Night Vale, The Read, My Favorite Murder*, and *2 Dope Queens* are a handful of examples of the variety of podcasts out there; each is a show with its own distinct take on the medium. No matter your interest and no matter your presentational style, you can make podcasts work for you.

A ZILLION COOL REASONS WHY YOU SHOULD START A PODCAST RIGHT THIS SECOND BUT NOT LIKE *RIGHT* THIS SECOND BECAUSE YOU'RE READING THIS BOOK

THEY'RE (USUALLY) EVERGREEN

Since the content of a podcast is often preplanned and more dictated by the style of the show than fast-moving Internet trends, podcast episodes don't grow stale as easily as, say, YouTube videos about fidget spinners. The *How Did This Get Made?* group, which mocks terrible retro movies, will be as relevant decades from now as they are today because cheesy movies deserving mockery will still deserve that mockery in the future.

THEY'RE INTIMATE

Podcasts are people talking directly to your ears, or, if you're wearing headphones, it's like they're talking directly inside your head. When you couple that with the conversational flow of most podcasts, it creates a format that feels very cozy, making it easy for listeners to kick back and unwind.

PODCAST LISTENERS ARE AN AUDIENCE EAGER FOR MATERIAL

Most people who listen to podcasts are also doing something they want to be distracted from, like driving to work, folding laundry, or battling back the endless demonic horde. Since your listeners are partially occupied doing something else, it means they're often going to be more forgiving about the occasional dull moments. Plus, in this age of increasingly ubiquitous multitasking, it's a godsend to have entertainment that can be consumed casually and easily while completing less-entertaining tasks.

IT'S EASY TO GET STARTED

The only things you need to start a podcast are a microphone, a hosting platform, and the will to make your idea into a reality.

IT'S EASY TO MAINTAIN

Keeping up your podcast doesn't require the escalating costs of inventory stock, nor do you have to worry about chasing trends the same way a YouTube series might, as your audience is going to skew older and will generally be there specifically for *you* rather than because your video autoplayed by accident. Also, since any on-camera work you do will be superfluous, you don't have to worry about the inevitable ravages of time wearing your flesh down to the skeletal nothings we all become!

IT'S STILL A FAIRLY NEW MEDIUM

Television, movies, and books all have legacies stretching back decades or even centuries. Video games, despite being pretty new to humanity from a nonlinear, nonsubjective viewpoint of time, are practically ancient compared to podcasts. The nascence of podcasts lends itself to innovation. If you've got a bold new idea for a kind of podcast you think no one has done before, odds are good that you're right. Sure, in the decades to come, podcasting innovations will be fewer and farther between. For now, innovate away, *mon frere.**

MOST, IF NOT ALL, OF YOUR WORK
CAN BE DONE IN YOUR PAJAMAS

No matter your job, if you can do it in your pajamas, things are probably pretty good.

---

* French for "my frere."

WORDS FROM WORKING NERDS

Troy Benjamin, author of books and comics, producer of feature films, former DVD-bonus-content producer, and fanboy who fills all his free time with endless projects like fansites, newsletters, and podcasts

How/when did you get started in your line/s of work?

Walking through the halls of the Loyola Marymount film school, I saw a generic print-out posting on the walls that simply said "Did you like the movie *Groundhog Day*?" and nothing else, except an e-mail address. Of course, being the huge Harold Ramis and *Ghostbusters* fan that I am, I was intrigued and reached out to the e-mail. It turned out it was producer Trevor Albert looking for a few good interns, and luckily I made the cut. I think it helped that his current assistant knew of the *Ghostbusters* fansite I had been running since junior high. So I worked for almost a year as an intern, eventually becoming Trevor's assistant, and from there he introduced me to a good number of the connections and colleagues I've worked with to this day.

What has surprised you most about your line of work?

I would have to say the most surprising thing I seem to encounter frequently is an unwillingness to take chances, despite a lot of people always claiming they're looking to do something "outside the box." I also think it's surprising that storytelling and how we create and consume content has been evolving and changing so rapidly that it's presenting so many wonderful opportunities, but there's a certain amount of trying to get people to catch up.

What tool could you not do without in your work?

I'd be lost without my Zoom H4N audio recorder. I'm a horrible note-taker, and my memory is so selective, it's embarrassing. I can't remember names or dates (except the release dates for *Star Wars* and *Ghostbusters*, for some reason), so making sure I don't miss anything during interviews is key.

What do you find most enjoyable about doing podcasts?

I have to tell you, I'm so glad Chris and I have been doing the *Ghostbusters Interdimensional Crossrip* podcast. The podcast feeds a couple desires I continue to enjoy: lengthy conversations about a movie that came out almost thirty-five years ago, and conversing and dissecting the topic with filmmakers and artisans in a long interview format.

How do you go about getting feedback on something like a podcast, where you don't necessarily have the reactions of a live audience to work with?

For better or worse, social media gives you instant feedback as if there were a live audience. If someone doesn't like something, they're pretty quick to tell you. If they enjoyed something, sometimes they'll chime in as well, and that always makes you feel pretty good. I'll leave it to the sociologists to unpack why Internet culture always seems to veer toward vocalizing the negative and sitting silent on the positive, but it's been interesting to observe and be on the receiving end.

Are there any particular obstacles you feel you've had to overcome to get where you are?

Money. I mean, it sounds really cynical, but it's true. It's extremely difficult to monetize a lot of these things. [That] is not to say I'm looking to finance a four-car garage to fill with a fleet of pristine DeLoreans, but you do have to pay rent and put food on the table.

A good friend of mine has an interesting perspective on all these projects, like the books, podcasts, etc.—because they're being done in the name of love, as soon as they are monetized they can also take on the baggage of being "just a job."* On the one hand, it would be great if all the fan-based projects you're doing because you love and enjoy producing [them] paid the bills. On the other hand, you don't want to lose that feeling of excitement and enthusiasm that fuels a lot of these projects.

What tips do you have for beating procrastination?

A producer I really admire taught me an incredibly good lesson: If there's something you can do, do it right now. Don't wait. If you need to pick up the phone and call someone, do it right that instant. Otherwise, you'll be apt to procrastinate and it'll never happen. Or it will somehow snowball and accumulate this meniscus around it, making it a more difficult task.

---

* This is not an uncommon phenomenon—in psychology, we refer to this as the *overjustification effect*, where increased *extrinsic* (external) motivation leads to decreased *intrinsic* (internal) motivation. It's definitely not universal, but it can happen, and it's something you'll need to be aware of and fight against as you find success.

To a certain extent, procrastination can be your worst enemy. With the demand for content as high as it is now, and with the amount of people who want to create that content increasing in numbers on a daily basis, there's a certain competitiveness that should fuel you. You have to be proactive. If you don't do this, someone else will.

And honestly, it helps to have a gym partner. You know, the person who is going to shame you in the morning if you skip meeting them at 6:00 a.m. at the gym to exercise. Having Chris and my wife to hold me accountable in releasing a weekly show without missing an episode release helps immensely.

Any tips or closing thoughts for newcomers looking to get into the business?

Be patient but persistent. Opportunities will pop up when you least expect them, and you have to be open to those when they present themselves. But you have to be patient until those opportunities arise. If you're passionate about something, let that fuel you.

STARTING POINT: PODCASTS

Okay, now that you're sold on the format and the idea of working in your pajamas, there are a few things you'll need to take care of before you can become a superstar podcaster driving a flying car and throwing thousand-dollar bills everywhere.

INVEST IN YOUR EQUIPMENT

While you can get your podcast started with naught more than a mic, if you want to make a *good* podcast, one that sounds professional and will keep bringing people back, you'll need to invest some time and understanding into the tools of the trade, such as:

- **A good gyat-dang microphone:** Since the only stimulus your audience will be receiving is auditory, it's worth every cent to get the best microphone you can. No one wants to listen to buzzing static and volume that's whisper-quiet one moment and screaming the next. Yeti microphones are generally pretty solid, as are several of the Audio-Technica mics, but your mileage will vary depending on your voice and recording location.* Broadly speaking, microphones come in two elemental varieties: *condenser* and *dynamic*. Condenser mics will generally give you better sound if you have a quiet environment to record in, but they pick up background noise like crazy. Dynamic mics are cheaper and won't pick up background noise as much, but the sound quality of what you do get is probably not going to be as good.

- **A microphone pop filter:** Any brand will do, really. You just need something decent that will soften out the harshness of your speech so your *P*s don't pop so hard and the little clicks and ticks don't come through so loudly.

---

* Full disclosure: None of the brands in this book have paid me to advertise for them. It's a weird era we live in, when people are so shifty in their advertising that I have to have a disclaimer basically saying I don't need a disclaimer.

- **WordPress:** If you need somewhere to build your site, it's hard to go wrong with a WordPress site (it's what I've used for years). Other services like Wix® and Squarespace® are also solid choices for site making.

- **Skype®:** Most podcast guests are already going to be familiar with Skype, which cuts out some of the potential technical snafus when showtime comes. Plus Skype makes it very easy to set up conference calls in the likely event that you/your cohosts/your guest are not all in the same location.

- **Ardour:** This flexible recording program gives you the power to set it up as you need, regardless of what operating system your computer runs on. Audacity is another good choice for all your recording and editing needs. Google Hangouts™ are another viable option.

- **FeedBurner®:** a web feed-management provider that makes it fairly painless to get your podcast uploaded to iTunes and the like

Remember that this is a business, and as with any business, you need to spend money to make money. Fortunately, you don't have to spend much money to start a podcast—you should be able to get high-quality equipment for a couple hundred bucks. It may be tempting to go a little cheap when getting started, but critical pieces of equipment such as microphones are *not* the place to cut corners. If your audio sounds like garbage, no one will want to listen and you'll be wasting your time.

PICK A TOPIC YOU'RE PASSIONATE ABOUT

If you're not into baseball, don't host a baseball podcast. If you don't think *Star Wars* is amazing, don't agree to cohost *Wookiee to Wookiee*. If you don't like to argue, don't do a podcast about re-watching every *Star Trek* series to figure out which captain is best.* A podcast lives and dies by the energy and drive of

---

* The correct answer, of course, is Cap'n Crunch.

its hosts, so if you can't muster up the enthusiasm to do variations of the same topic over and over, your podcast will suffer a quick and meaningless death.

As with any creative endeavor, think through the podcasts you enjoy and consider what you can learn from them: Do you like the topic or the format? Do you like the host's informative style, or the cohost's wandering comedy? Is there a type of podcast you'd love to hear, but no one else is doing? Which podcasting trends are starting to take off, and which ones are you sick of already? If you don't have a clue how to answer these questions, you need to listen to more podcasts before starting one.

SOME WELL-KNOWN PODCASTS AND THE GENRES ONE MIGHT CATEGORIZE THEM UNDER SHOULD ONE FEEL INCLINED TO DO SO

Comedy podcasts are focused on, first and foremost, delivering the laughs.
- **Examples:** *Spontaneanation; My Brother, My Brother and Me; 2 Dope Queens; With Special Guest Lauren Lapkus; You Made It Weird with Pete Holmes; The Adventure Zone*

Pop culture podcasts endeavor to better understand popular culture and its effect on the people who absorb it.
- **Examples:** *How Did This Get Made?, The Read, Hollywood Babble-On, Doug Loves Movies, Ghostbusters Interdimensional Crossrip, Sistah Speak, Harry Potter and the Sacred Text*

Gaming podcasts discuss the trends and impact of video games.
- **Examples:** *Giant Bombcast, 8-4 Play, The Patch, Gamers With Jobs, Three Moves Ahead*

Education and history podcasts draw from real-life events and people of the past to teach us a li'l something for today.
- **Examples:** *Serial; StarTalk Radio Show with Neil deGrasse Tyson; BackStory with the American History Guys; Stuff You Missed in History Class; The History Chicks; 1001 Heroes, Legends, Histories & Mysteries; Radiolab*

Horror podcasts inject a double dose of spooky right into your eardrums
- **Examples:** *Welcome to Night Vale, Lore, Pseudopod, The NoSleep Podcast, Tales To Terrify*

Advice podcasts, as you might expect, offer advice. Generally, these podcasts rely on listener stories and questions to generate their content, so they can be difficult to get up and running if you don't have anyone asking for advice.

By doing an advice podcast, you will be telling people how to live their lives, and, depending on the topic, that may veer into dangerous territory. If you have a tech advice show telling people how to deal with computer problems, you're probably in the clear. Most advice podcasts, however, focus on life advice, often hosted by people whose only qualification is life experience. I can't recommend that people without professional backgrounds give advice to others on life, love, and health, as it's likely they will give bad or misguided advice. If you're going to do an advice podcast, do it in an area you're well-educated in.

WORDS FROM WORKING NERDS

Justin McElroy, one of the titular brothers behind *My Brother, My Brother and Me* and *The Adventure Zone* podcasts, YouTube's Monster Factory, Polygon editor and cofounder, and all-around entertainer

When I was thirteen, I was on a local kids' TV news show called *Kid's Mag*. While I was in high school, the creator of that show and I wrote a video-game column called *Gameview*. I started writing about video games for a site called HuntingtonNews. net after that and then I started working full-time in newspapers after college and freelanced about video games on the side for [publications] like *Official Playstation Magazine* and *PC Gamer* and others that no longer exist, because video game magazines don't exist anymore. Basically, I got in while the getting was good. From there I got a job at *Joystiq* and I started doing the *Joystiq Podcast*. I joined with them after they'd done ten episodes, and we sort of built that show up and built an audience for it. In 2010 we spun off *MBMBAM* [*My Brother, My Brother and Me*] and the other shows kind of spun off *MBMBAM*.

What is your daily routine like?

It varies wildly. I don't really have set times for hardly any of the projects we do; we schedule everything ad hoc, as wild as that is. An average day for me usually starts with trying to comb through my e-mail. During the morning, I try to do recording early in the day, between ten o'clock and two o'clock—I find that's creatively the easiest to deal with. We do a lot more meetings than we used to with, like, our merch partners, and stuff like that. The evening is usually when I've got a window, between five thirty and eight o'clock, where I'm with my kids and it's dinner, baths, and bed. After that is the one time my wife and I are free, so it's the time when we tend to work on *Sawbones*-related stuff, either recording the show, researching the show, or working on the *Sawbones* book.

What has surprised you the most about your line of work?

That I'm able to make a living doing it. That sounds like I'm kidding, but honestly, when I was younger I had no idea you could do this kind of work. I just didn't know this was a career choice people had. I think the biggest surprise to me is that we were able to find an audience—I didn't understand that it could happen for me until it did. I think once we started building our live touring business, that was the first time it sank in. Like, seeing that we had a venue with three thousand people who were all there to see us was one very humbling but also wild thing.

Your work has inspired others to be creative, with everything from other podcasts to people getting tattoos referencing specific episodes of your shows. How does it feel to know you have that kind of impact?

[It's been] humbling and overwhelming and has filled me with no small amount of paranoia. I still don't think of myself as particularly exceptional—I would extend the label of "exceptional" to my brothers and wife and the people I work with. I honestly spend a lot of time waiting for the other shoe to drop and expecting people to wise up that I'm not that great. I think that's probably a healthy response?

What are some of the challenges you face with ongoing projects like podcasts?

I think the bigger challenge is trying to infuse stuff with fresh energy, like we've been doing *MBMBAM* for a bunch of years now, and it's a challenge to try to make it feel fresh every time.

Like, with *The Adventure Zone*, which we still do, we ended the story line that we were working on, and I think that was sort of a natural realization that we'd reached the end of the road with that story, that we'd told it. Eventually people move on, they outgrow stuff, and I think the audience moved with us.

Are there any particular obstacles you feel you've had to overcome to get where you are?

I am limited by geography a lot of times. Where I live is not an entertainment hub. There are probably a lot of opportunities I could pursue if I lived in NYC or LA that I don't pursue. [My location] keeps me from pursuing those opportunities. That and there's not much in the way of collaborators in my area, so I don't organically meet the people to do stuff with that I would in a larger area.

We developed a friendship with the guys who do the podcast *The Worst Idea of All Time*. We met them at LA PodCon and developed a friendship, and we make a podcast together where we watch *Paul Blart: Mall Cop 2* every year at Thanksgiving and then do an episode about it as an annual event. But we met them at a thing and developed a relationship and made a thing with them. I think I would do more of that kind of collaboration if I did live somewhere where other people were doing this kind of work.

Who or what are your inspirations?

My dad is probably the biggest. He was a radio deejay for forty-some odd years doing the morning shift, and he's someone who really wants to make people happy. Seeing the way he handled [his career] and his priorities is a big inspiration to me. I feel like a lot of the people . . . I worry about idolizing people I don't know, because it seems like a lot of them end up being bad dudes and bad women—more bad dudes, let's be honest—so I don't tend to have a lot of people that I feel that way about necessarily, I tend to keep [my inspirations limited] more to people that I know. My wife, too, is a big inspiration to me to keep my head on straight and prioritize stuff and convince me to take opportunities when I feel that imposter syndrome we talked about. She's the one who convinces me of my own worth.

What tips might you recommend to newcomers looking to get into the business?

Here's the most valuable thing I can tell anybody. . . . It's a brief story, so begging your forgiveness: Bob Thompson plays piano for [national radio show] *Mountain Stage*. I was talking to him when I was much younger and told him I was trying to get into entertainment. He told me that when he was getting started, he went into . . . I think it was Capital Records, and he had a demo. [Capital Records] listened to it and said, "This is great stuff, but we can't do anything with you." He didn't understand, and they said, "This is great, but there are ten other people who can do this exact thing. Come back to us when you know what it is you do that nobody else does."

That's the sort of thing that I think is extremely valuable in my line of work. It took me a long time to figure out, and a lot of people don't figure this out first when they really should, and that is: What is the thing that you do better than anybody else, or that nobody else can do? I believe that everyone has that something, not necessarily an entertainment thing but the something their life has uniquely positioned them to make. But I think that until you figure out what that thing is, you're going to have a tough time.

I mentioned the freelance stuff I did, but the undercurrent of that is the dozens of job applications and freelance pitches that went nowhere or took forever to come to fruition. I'm kind of surprised, knowing myself, that I stuck with it as I did. The interesting thing for me is that I really wasn't ready when I was sending those pitches. The important thing was that I was still working on my own stuff, trying to hone my craft, and I think if I'd gotten some of those opportunities earlier, I wouldn't have been ready for them.

PICK A NAME THAT'S CLEVER WITHOUT BEING *SO* CLEVER, IT'S NOT DESCRIPTIVE

Nerdist cohost Matt Mira had a long-running podcast called *Talk Salad and Scrambled Eggs*, which was a series analyzing the merits and missteps of the television show *Frasier*. While the name may be amusingly clever to *Frasier* fans, it made it hard to draw in new listeners who weren't familiar enough with *Frasier* to know its closing theme by heart. Most folks probably took one look at the name and thought it was a cooking show, which might be why the *full* title is actually *Talk Salad and Scrambled Eggs: Frasier Reconsidered*.

People need to have some idea as to what your show is about. Whatever your given topic, find some kind of cheeky wordplay you can use that will catch the eye while still being descriptive. Also, know that if your podcast is one about the general state of geekdom, you're going to have a hard time finding a unique name, because there are only so many clever permutations of the words *geek* or *nerd*.

THE NEXT STEP: PODCASTS

OR

TRAINING UNDER THE FREEZING WATERFALL OF THE INTERNET TO STRENGTHEN YOUR PODCAST CHI

All right! You're ready to get your podcast going, eh? Well, despite the simplicity of entry to the podcast game, getting good at podcasting requires a serious investment of effort on your part. If you ever want to crack iTunes' Top Twenty (or Ten, or Five), you need to hit the books. Well, *the* book. This book. Which you already have. Anyway, here's some ways to help make your podcast better.

LISTEN TO YOUR OWN VOICE
Since our mouths and ears are all connected to the meaty things we call our heads, the sound waves of our speech vibrate our eardrums differently than

they do everyone else, so we don't hear what we actually sound like. A good rule of thumb is to realize that your voice probably sounds higher than what you're used to. Record yourself speaking in a variety of tones to get a feel for what you truly sound like; if you're going to be using an auditory medium, you'll need a better understanding of what you're working with.

Also know that not everyone is blessed with a nice speaking voice. Whether you're gravel-voiced from smoking or that old witch's curse has left you with a cat's meow instead of human vocal tones, you may face some extra difficulties in doing a podcast. Again, *listen* to your voice. Adjust as much as you can to sound as smooth and nice as possible (and if you smoke, well, y'know, *don't*). Taking voice lessons probably isn't a bad idea, either.

TRAIN IN THE ART OF CONVERSATION

Conversing with the beast known as "hyoo-mann" isn't always the easiest. While much of your podcast is probably going to be you bullshitting around with your friends, you'll need the occasional guest and you may not always know those guests ahead of time. Make the effort to become a better conversationalist. Practice active listening, try to focus on the positives of both your guest and your topic, maintain speaker balance between yourself and the other people on your show, and don't be overly critical of the other speakers.

A conversation is a gentle, sloshing back-and-forth; it's the ocean, not a fire hose. Don't drown your guests and cohosts. Get in a little rowboat and paddle around with them.

LAUNCH WITH SEVERAL EPISODES AT THE READY

On launch day, start by posting three to five episodes, publish multiple times a week for the first few weeks, and have a buffer of several additional episodes at the ready for the coming weeks. If people listen to your first episode, they're hopefully going to want to listen to more. If you already *have* more ready for them, you just got yourself a subscriber. If they don't have anything else to listen to, odds are high that they'll get distracted by cat memes and forget about your show instead of subscribing.

LAUNCH BIG AND STAY BIG FOR THE FIRST TWO WEEKS

The first couple of weeks of a podcast are an important crucible, as they determine whether you can land yourself in the New and Noteworthy section of iTunes and other podcast directories. Do your best to draw as much attention to yourself as you can those first two weeks, whether it's through flooding your social media and mailing list, doing mass giveaways, being a guest on other people's podcasts/blogs/video channels, streaming constantly from your own video channel, or dressing up as a podcast-themed supervillain and robbing a bank.*

GET A GOOD INTRO AND OUTRO

Intros and outros should be short, punchy, and professional. While there are many areas in professional nerddom where it's a good idea to rely on your partially skilled friends to do something for you for free, your podcast intro and outro aren't among them. These are the first and last things your listeners will hear; your intro is your one shot to get people listening, and your outro is the last thing they'll be thinking about once your podcast is over. Shell out a few bucks to get professionally made music and voice talent to record what you need done.

Also keep the intro short—thirty seconds or less. You've only got a few seconds to hook people in, so make it count. If your intro is an overblown affair, your potential listeners will grow bored and move on to the next thing that ain't you.

PLAN YOUR EPISODES AHEAD OF TIME

Podcasts take a considerable amount of set-up and coordination. Before you start on your podcasting adventure, figure out what sort of publishing schedule you feel is feasible, factoring in the difficulty of wrangling the many cohosts and guests you need for every episode.

---

* Don't do that; a podcast-themed supervillain would be really lame.

I love TV, and I've been a TV junkie since childhood. I'd been listening to podcasts for a year or so, and after talking with my co-creator and cohost, Sistah J, about the latest events on a few reality shows, we decided to start our own podcast. We wanted to talk about the things that were important to us, namely the portrayal of people of color on television and in movies. We created our first podcast in the summer of 2007, and we've been podcasting continually since then.

What do you like most about podcasting?

How fulfilled it makes me. I can express myself through the podcast in ways I never thought possible. I can connect with listeners—our "Family," as we call them—in a truly sincere and direct way.

With many nerdy projects, such as podcasts, one could conceivably continue more or less indefinitely. How do you know when it's time to finish up a project and let it go?

Our podcast is a bit different from other "recap-style" podcasts. For example, we have the same seasons as the shows we discuss. As for ending a podcast series altogether, we know it's time to end when we no longer enjoy watching the show. Unfortunately, we've ended several podcast series before the actual television show ended, for that very reason.

What do you find most enjoyable about doing podcasts?

I find the interaction with our Family, aka the listeners, the most enjoyable part of podcasting. We have a thriving private Facebook group bustling with activity. I love spending time in the group chatting with people. We've also started in-person events we call "The Sistah Speak Family Reunion" located in several cities, where we spend time with our listeners and celebrate one another.

How do you manage the feedback for your podcast?

We started our podcasts reading every piece of feedback we received. Of course, at the beginning there were just a few e-mails. Now, on our most popular shows, we may receive fifty or sixty e-mails and voice mails per episode. We still take the time to read, listen to, and acknowledge the contents of each one, which does make for some long-ass podcasts. I believe this allows us to connect with our listeners in a truly organic way, and it allows them to be a part of each podcast. Having our Facebook group and Twitter feeds (as well as other social media) also allows us to receive instant feedback. We're lucky in that our Family members are never shy about sending feedback.

Are there any particular obstacles you feel you've had to overcome to get where you are?

The main obstacle I've overcome was having the confidence in my abilities to learn how to podcast. Another was whether people would want to hear what I had to say. The technical side of podcasting was daunting at first, especially ten years ago. At that time, there weren't as many resources available as there are nowadays. Having a cohost to bounce ideas off and having interesting topics to discuss made producing continuous podcast episodes a bit easier.

CONNECT, CHILL, AND BE COOL

Internet audiences *love* interaction. Interact with people through social media, offer video hangouts or chats as subscriber content, answer every not-creepy question someone submits to your Facebook inbox. Every person you interact with is more likely to come back to you in the future.

RE-LISTEN TO YOUR EPISODES AND DO SOME BASIC EDITING BEFORE POSTING THEM ONLINE

Dead air, static-y crackles, discussions about bathroom breaks, burps, farts, sneezes, coughs, and the bubbling of your clone vats are major turn-offs to potential listeners. Listen, edit, and excise them from your recording.

BE SMART ABOUT LENGTH

Most podcast episodes come in at approximately an hour (or less). Bigger, more established podcasts will often go over that amount because they've got an accumulated audience who can't get enough of their content. Until you hit that point, you need to give potential fans enough to wet their whistles without going so overboard that they grow tired of a particular episode.

FIND WAYS TO MAKE MONEY FROM THE SAME THING MORE THAN ONCE

Any video, any article, any podcast, any *work* you do can likely be reused for fun, profit, and efficiency. Run a blog to support your podcast and post your episodes through your site with a paragraph or two of description/post-episode thoughts to go along with it. Or create a short vlog to go with each new episode of your podcast and create a link in the video description. You're the one working your buns off, and you're going to be doing a lot of that work for free, so it's in your best interest to find ways of maximizing the profits for your efforts. Just do be mindful not to overextend the same content, as you will have fans who follow you on more than one platform and they'll tire of seeing the same podcast episode pop up in their feed four times in rapid succession.

MAKE A PLAN AND LEARN TO IMPROVISE

Knowing how to improvise means knowing how to work within the flow of a conversation to create something. Many wannabe podcasters try to go *au naturel* in their conversations and don't prepare. Guess what? Those conversations are rancid *garbage*. Create an outline for each episode covering the topics you want to hit, questions you want to ask, and stories you want told, and be ready to make changes when something interesting comes up mid-conversation. Improvisational skills help any podcast move more smoothly, whether the tone is light-hearted and fun or dead-freaking-serious.

TALK TO YOUR GUESTS!

When you bring on folks to talk about whatever it is that makes them noteworthy, don't ignore them so you and your regular cohosts can talk about whatever's on your mind. Your listeners get you and your team every episode; when you've got a guest, it's your job to make them shine. Not only will it make your guest feel welcome and more likely to recommend your show to other potential guests, it will also make *their* fans feel that their time was well-spent and add a spicy element of variety to each episode.

TAG YOUR EPISODES

In the iTunes story, in your RSS feed, on your site, and in the sound file of the podcast itself, tag each li'l goober of an episode with a few smart, SEO keywords to help the people who would like your show find it.

HAVE GOOD COVER ART

Often your cover art is the very first impression people will get of your podcast; is it something fun, inviting, and informative, or a blown-up 120-pixel JPEG of your dog with some words splattered across it? No, don't answer. It was a rhetorical question and this is a book.

SUBMIT TO PODCAST DIRECTORIES AND AGGREGATORS

Podcast Alley, Podcast Pickle, and PodcastDirectory.com are a few of the sites and services you can use to help disseminate your podcast to the 'net for free.

POST PULL QUOTES AND SOUND BITES FOR EASY REPOSTING

Find a quote from your episodes that you consider attention-grabbing, whether it's a good joke, an intelligent musing, or something wildly out of context. Build an image containing that quote and post it online; when others see it, they'll be more likely to comment/repost what you've done, increasing audience reach and visibility. You can also do the same thing with quick sound bites of your episode's audio, but know that sound bites don't tend to have as high an absorption rate since it takes more time to listen to them than it does to read a quick quote.

AS ALWAYS, ENCOURAGE PEOPLE TO SHARE, SUBSCRIBE, AND RATE YOUR WORK

I know, it's tiring to always ask your audience to share/subscribe/rate/like your work, but social media engagement is a key element to any nerdy career. So suck it up, buttercup, and do it!

An easy way to get quick iTunes reviews is to create a nice, clean URL like *YourPodcast'sName.com/Review* and have the URL redirect to your iTunes review page, then plug that sucker at the end of every single episode.

MONETIZE SMARTLY

Podcasters have a somewhat easier time monetizing their content, as there's an audience expectation that some advertising will have to occur to keep the lights on. Sponsored ad breaks before/during/after your show work well; once you're a bit more established and can impress potential sponsors with your numbers, sell slots of time wherein you advertise for them.

Generally speaking, it's much better for *you* to be the one doing the advertising, as you can add a bit of your own personal flair to the proceedings and the audience will respond better to someone from your team than from a stranger advertising at them. With that in mind, only advertise products and services you believe in; don't promote anything you feel is suspicious, immoral, or unethical.

Crowdfunded subscription platforms like Patreon lend themselves to podcasting. Offering ad-free downloads to those who pay for your podcast, either as one-time purchases or through small membership fees, is a good way to get additional income at little cost to yourself. If your podcast works as a live performance, do it live and charge for tickets. You can also just flat-out ask for donations, especially early on when it's understood that you're building your brand.

You can use your podcast to increase your revenue through other services you provide, advertising your YouTube channel, blog, web design service, side gig as a monster hunter, etc.

Once you're very established, you might consider selling masterclasses in podcasting to teach newcomers how to improve their shows, offering to listen to and critique their work in order to better them. This can fall into a bit of a murky area, as there are a number of unscrupulous people on the Internet who offer such services while providing very little in the way of useful feedback. I would recommend you only do this if you are extremely experienced and confident in your ability to help others get their podcasts to the same level as yours.

Podcasting isn't for everyone. There are those of us who prefer the quiet and solitude of visual work, who enjoy being alone for long stretches of time, who would rather create breathtaking imagery than living soundscapes. I speak of the paint-spattered beast, the one with the hand gnarled into a claw holding a tablet pen—*the digital artist.*

CHAPTER EIGHT

ART AND COMICS

F ine artists have a professional tradition stretching back to the dawn of human civilization. As with all things, however, the Internet has changed the ways in which artists operate. Today's artists don't have to sit around waiting for someone to discover their work or suffer through the endless parade of art shows and auctions and art battles where artists paint to summon massive devil-beasts that fight for the amusement of the elite bourgeoisie. Thanks to the power of social media and crowdfunding, it's never been easier for aspiring artists to draw what they love and get it into the hands of people who love it too.

TYPES OF NERDY ARTISTES*

Art is an infinite, intangible, undefinable concept. What makes something art? Is it intent? Execution? Audience reaction? Pretentious people have argued about this for centuries. In our case, it's a lot easier to define what we're talking about since we're focusing on nerdy art—any art with a geeky, scholarly, pop-culture-y flair.

There are two primary types of nerdy, professional artists we'll be discussing here. The first is the **webcomic artist**, someone who uses the Internet as the platform for their sequential art. Webcomics are the hieroglyphics of the Internet, providing an early means of expression and notoriety in the earliest days of the 'net.

Most comics tend to lean toward the nerdier side of things, and webcomics even more so. Most of the longest-running comics are about nerds or nerdy topics—when webcomics really began taking off in the late '90s

---

* An *artiste* is exactly like an artist, only fancier because of the extra E.

and early 2000s, you couldn't click through two pages without tripping over someone's comic of two guys on a couch playing video games.

Webcomics are a difficult road, as they require high levels of planning and dedication, with the GoLion's share of the work falling on the artist (or writer/ artist, as the case often is). The format offers a high degree of freedom for delivering personal stories, thoughts, and jokes; it's the modern, digital evolution of yesterday's print comics, political comics, and cutting-edge underground comix.

Should you desire to become a webcomic artist, you'll first need to plan what type of comic you intend to create, beyond limitations like character, genre, or setting. Broadly speaking, webcomics fall into three categories:

One-off gag comics eschew continuity and character in favor of making the joke that needs made at any given time.

➧ **Examples:** *Saturday Morning Breakfast Cereal, XKCD, Chainsawsuit*

Loose continuity comics often feature the same characters or places without worrying too much about the specifics. *Penny Arcade*'s Gabe and Tycho have both died countless times, yet they're still around in all their puffy-haired glory. Webcomics with a loose continuity reach a happy medium between freedom to express and continuity of ideas.

➧ **Examples:** *Penny Arcade, Whomp!,* the brilliant and oh-so-NSFW *Oglaf*

Continuous story comics are the sort of comics that require planning from their creators—it's tough trying to plot out character and story arcs without knowing where you'll be five or more years down the road. Still, this devotion to structure brings with it an ever-more-devoted fanbase. Fans know and appreciate when you put in the extra time it takes to make a webcomic with a continuous story, so you'll have an easier time drawing in a larger fanbase.

➧ **Examples:** *Questionable Content, Gunnerkrigg Court, Paranormal Activity, Megatokyo*

An oddity of making a webcomic, however, is that sticking with the same comic means those early, eyesore pages are going to linger around forever and will be a click of the "First Page" button away for every visitor to your site. If you're posting through a social network, that's not as likely to be an issue since the format's different, but most comics found through social media platforms are of the insular-gag variety, not an ongoing story, so there's no need for people to read from the beginning because there's no continuity to worry about.

WHEN TO MURDER THE MONSTER FOR GOOD

One issue faced by nearly every creative working on the same project for a long time is fatigue. There's a reason Sir Arthur Conan Doyle tried to kill off Sherlock Holmes—he was sick of writing about him. Odds are good that even if you become monstrously successful, you'll grow sick of writing and drawing the same thing. So what do you do when your success has left you feeling stagnant? When do you murder the monster your work has become? There are a few options:

- Finish your series the moment you feel that itch, and go out with a big, dignified bang. Leave your fans satisfied, wanting more, and eager for your next project.

- Write and draw side projects that don't pay the bills but leave you creatively fulfilled.

- Take long breaks. This is risky because you *will* lose some audience every time you go on hiatus.

- Collaborate. Work with other people to help reinvigorate your creativity.

- Reboot the sucker and start anew.

- Drag things out soullessly, unhappily making money at something you don't find fulfilling.

- Abandon your work with nary a word, telling your friends that you intend to get back to it someday while knowing deep in your heart that you never will. This is the option chosen by most content creators.

The second type of nerdy artist is the **fan artist**, someone who focuses their work on cleverly reimagining and reproducing recognizable icons. These are the artists who spend their days drawing gender-swapped Super Mario Bros., or Japanese Wall Scroll versions of *Ghostbusters,* or steampunk Batman, or regular ol' pictures of pop culture characters drawn in the artist's unique style. Fan art is the place many nerdy artists get their start, and many find the field so fun and interesting that they spend most of their time there, letting their style grow while they find meaningful, beautiful ways to represent their favorite characters.

It should be mentioned that making money from fan art is treated as a bit of a gray area, legally speaking. At any fan convention, you'll see countless artists selling fan art of pop culture characters, but few, if any, have the legal permission to do so. Most big companies aren't interested in cracking down on artists making a few bucks off of their IPs (intellectual property), as it's not worth their time and money, plus it makes them look really petty. So if you're selling art of licensed characters, then you'll probably be fine; it's once you start, say, doing large-scale production of unlicensed characters, like T-shirts with the Wonder Woman logo on them, that you will run into trouble.

STARTING POINT: NERDY ART*

If you've decided to go into the field of nerdy art, odds are good that you've already got a decent idea of the sort of tools you'll need—things like:

- **Tablet with digital pen:** Wacom tablets come highly recommended. Regardless of what tablet you pick up, you'll want to fidget with the sensitivity quite a bit until it feels right; this will take fine-tuning from you.

- **Programs:** Adobe Photoshop is the gold standard for many digital artists, but it comes at a serious price tag. Adobe Illustrator is solid, but it isn't essential. There are numerous free art and comics

---

* You'll notice this section primarily focuses on your pen-and-paper sort of art, not as much sculpting and whatnot since I pretty well covered that way back in the crafting chapter (page 101).

programs you might want to consider, such as Manga Studio, Artweaver, Inkscape®, and Krita. These programs vary in terms of versatility and richness of design; some of the products you'll make with free programs will *look* like they were made with free programs.

◆ While **image scanners** are definitely helpful tools, they aren't as crucial as they used to be. If your work is mostly digital, you don't really have to worry about translating physical work into digital, because it's already done.

◆ **A decent computer:** Photoshop and other art programs can be serious memory hogs. For your digital work, you're going to want to have a computer strong enough to handle the many layers and brushes of your work and the obsessively frequent saving you should be doing because things can crash at any moment. Computer speed can be an issue with Photoshop, as files can often be so large your computer slows to a painfully slow speeds, We're talking zombie-missing-its-lower-torso-and-feeling-kind-of-drowsy kind of crawl.

◆ **Pens:** Digital allows you to make as many mistakes as you want and to change your mind later. Physical mediums like inking teach you to bring a decisiveness to your marks, which allows you to work faster, better, and more often. Legendary comic book artist Sergio Aragonés (*Mad* magazine, *Groo the Wanderer*) blitzed his way through countless sketches at lightning speed due to the boldness of his movements. If you've ever been lucky enough to attend the Quick Draw panel at San Diego Comic-Con, you've probably been witness to the speed and humor of his art, the way he could slice an image onto a page like an ink-drenched samurai master. This speed, this precision of conveyance, only comes from years of practice using a bold medium like ink. Art is at its best when it lacks self-consciousness. Tommy Wiseau may not be the world's best actor, but, by Odin's beard, is he fearless in his expression, and as a result we got the unique wonderfulness of his film *The Room*.

- **Pencils:** Graphite and colored pencils come in a variety of shades, hardness, and darkness. A small pack with a handful of gradients is probably all you need; having too many gradients can make you waste your time trying to figure out if a pencil is the "right" pencil.

- **A sketch pad, preferably several:** Keep a pocket-size sketch pad with you wherever you go and sketch when the impulse seizes you. At home, use a larger sketch pad to work on variations of the same concept on one page; it will be easier for you to make comparisons between them.

- **A canvas, paint set, and brush set:** Painting isn't for everyone, as it takes a lot of prep and space and may not suit your style of art; that said, it forces you to work with impulsive decisions and hones your decisive element. Paintings also sell better than purely graphite pencil work.

KNOW THYSELF'S BUDGET

Art costs money to make. Digital art has a high up-front cost, with computers, tablets, and art programs being at a high price point but low maintenance cost once you've got what you need. Traditional media such as pencil, paint, and hedgehog excrement all have low costs of entry but continuous maintenance costs. Pencils break, paint dries, and hedgehogs aren't always pooping, so expect frequent art supply runs in your future. Plus, while digital art mostly takes up hard drive space to make and store, physical art requires materials that take up physical space as you use them.

Initially, it's going to be difficult to figure out exactly how much your monthly budget will be (and how much of it will be eaten up by supplies). For the pricier parts of your artistic toolset, I'd recommend asking friends and family for them as birthday/holiday gifts to take some of the sting out of your wallet.

CREATE A PRODUCTIVE WORKSPACE

Where are you going to create your art? At your home office? At a coffeehouse, so you can sip caffeine and look pretentious? Hanging upside-down in a cavern in South America? Wherever your workspace is going to be, try to make it as free from bad distractions as possible. I'm not talking about music or podcasts, as those can be good distractions for many artists by allowing them to focus part of their mind on what they're hearing and let their artistic side focus on the art itself. I'm talking about, say, random people walking by and talking to you, or YouTube/the Internet at large, both of which are distractions that require maintenance from you and pull you out of that delicious, ever-elusive *flow* (see page 10).

PRACTICE, PRACTICE, PRACTICE, THEN PRACTICE SOME MORE, THEN KEEP PRACTICING, THEN ONCE YOU'RE DONE PRACTICING YOU KEEP PRACTICING BECAUSE YOU'RE NEVER DONE GETTING BETTER

Every author with a published book has half a dozen more terrible books that will never see the light of day, and any artist creating gorgeous works of art will have a rogue's gallery of terrible garbage they made while practicing and learning their trade. Art skills can be picked up with enough time, and the skills you learn while painting or inking or drawing with graphite or using a particular program will frequently translate to another medium or program. All practice is worth your time, even if it doesn't result in a useable product in a medium you normally work with.

DON'T WASTE TIME FIDDLING WITH KNOBS

When I get a new game with character customization, I like to spend a lot of time tweaking the facial features, trying to see if my character will look cool in-game or like a troll doll with a flashlight stuffed under its chin. Sometimes this process takes so long I run out of time to actually play the game.

The same issue can happen to artists. Fiddling with custom nibs and brushes and paint combinations can be a productive use of your time; it can also be a way of losing yourself in the minutiae and not getting anything productive accomplished. Getting the work done and spending time practicing is much more important than wasting endless hours calibrating your tools until they're *juuuuuuuuuust* right. You'll intuitively get a feel for what you need as you're working.

WORDS FROM WORKING NERDS

Ronnie Filyaw, best known for writing and drawing the comic *Whomp!*

About seven and a half years ago, I became frustrated with trying to find a job that suited me. So while I was unemployed, I began drawing different comics to be posted on the Internet. The first two titles I attempted left me unsatisfied, but upon reading KC Green's *Gunshow*, I was inspired to try something new and absurd. I was happy with what I was creating, and it's the primary reason I stuck with it.

What is the process like for creating a webcomic?

I would say no such "average workday" exists for me. I will wake up in the morning very grumpy; then as I watch streaming videos on the Internet, I will fret over what joke I'm writing next. Once I've managed to work out a joke I think is acceptable, I will pull out my lap table and digitizing tablet and draw it. Usually, I'm listening to a podcast or watching a television show that doesn't require much of my attention while I work.

What has been most surprising about doing webcomics?

I believe I may be a special case, but I've been amazed at the niceness of my readers. Barring a minuscule percentage of outliers, I've received almost nothing but kind comments, e-mails, and tweets. My comics often joke about heavy topics like depression and suicide, but no one has ever said to me, "You shouldn't joke about that."

What's the hardest part of your job?

The greatest obstacle has been complacency. It is very, extremely, unfathomably easy to simply say, "I will not write a comic today." Today turns into tomorrow, and tomorrow becomes "ever again." I've managed, thanks to both the support of wonderful fans and a livable income, to push through those boundaries. *Whomp!* is the only project I've ever stuck with to such a satisfying degree. I am still prone to allowing projects to immediately fall by the wayside, but *Whomp!* is eternal for me.

What are the advantages and disadvantages of your medium?

The primary advantage of webcomics is that your comic can enter pretty much every Internet-connected computer in the world at the moment it is posted. You have the ability to reach into the nooks and crannies of society and pluck out the people to whom your comic resonates on a personal level. This is opposed to print comics, which reach the dwindling audience of people who would pick up an English-language newspaper, assuming you could even convince them to run a comic about farts and crying!

A disadvantage of working on the web is the gargantuan amount of competition. It is advantageous that anyone can make a webcomic, but that means *everyone* can make a webcomic. To defeat that disadvantage requires having not only a consistent schedule, but something special. You have to work thrice as hard as anyone else, and even then, you may not be able to create something to which people really respond.

Any parting advice for hopeful webcomic creators?

Don't quit your day job. I cannot express how important it is to put everything in your life before your webcomic. Do not leave your job. Do not neglect your family. Do not cancel social events (unless you really don't want to go). Some of the greatest authors wrote their books on the train to work. If your passion for the work is real, the time will find you. Now, with that bit of crushing discouragement out of the way, the most important comic to make is one inspired by something you love. For me, I love picking fun at myself, so that's what I do in my comics. Maybe someday I'll write a comic about thought-provoking space journeys!

THE NEXT STEP: NERDY ART

Once you've gotten your feet wet in ink, you're going to have a single, burning question on your mind, the same question artists have been asking of the world since the dawn of human civilization: How can I make some money so I can keep doing this?

CROWDFUNDING IS YOUR FRIEND

Crowdfunding platforms like Patreon and Gumroad enable artists to make steady income from their work. If you post regularly, particularly if you're working in the field of webcomics, it's a smart idea to quickly get on a crowdfunding platform. Sure, it'll feel odd having a Patreon with zero patrons for a while. Don't sweat it—you're setting things up for later, for after you've started building up your following. Start promoting those crowdfunding pages early and frequently.

STREAM YOUR ART

Streaming your artistic process makes for a surprisingly good, surprisingly easy show. Play some gentle music and get to drawing. Interact with fans if you want. Or don't. Talking about your process in real time is a good idea, as it'll help both your audience and you learn from what you're doing.

SELL ART TUTORIALS

Once you're a bit more established (and halfway kinda know what you're doing), try offering art tips. Working one-on-one with people is a more difficult proposition, as scheduling can be a pain and not everyone deals with criticism well. An easier route to go is to create prepackaged tutorials your subscribers/patrons can get regular access to. One week, offer an in-depth tutorial on how to draw hands, the next, how to draw hair, then tips on perspective, and so on. Make your tutorials friendly, informative, and, most importantly, easy to read. It sucks to get a great art tutorial you can't read because the artist has the penmanship of a white walker.

DIVERSIFY YOUR SKILLSET

As with every other type of nerdy living I discuss in this book, I recommend you diversify your skillset as an artist. Don't just bank on being successful through one type of art; you never know what will or won't take off at any given moment. Plus, studying more than one form of art makes you a stronger artist overall, giving you insight and techniques you can take from one field and apply to another.

TO CHEESECAKE, OR NOT TO CHEESECAKE?

In the artistic world, "cheesecake" art refers to images of women flaunting their sexy stuff. Drawing cheesecake and beefcake* art can be fun and positive, not to mention lucrative, but it's also a bit of a slippery slope. When it comes to erotic content, the Internet is a dang weird place. No matter what you draw, there will be people who demand you draw something more explicit and fetishy until you're so far outside your comfort zone you have to create contingency plans about how to hide your embarrassingly weird art from your parents in case you die suddenly.

Finding where you draw the line is important, as people who commission hyper-specific fetish art are often unreasonably demanding in their specificity (not to mention that their fetishes can be downright gross). Any artist would get exhausted from having to do fourteen versions of the same picture of Inspector Gadget being forcibly turned into a slice of deli cheese while wearing a diaper.

So should the sexy art route be one you wish to take, find a line and find it early. Don't take commissions for something you're uncomfortable drawing. Also, if you're going to focus on drawing sexy women, do it in a way that is more about celebrating the woman's command of her own sexuality and not so much about objectifying her.

BEING DEPENDABLE IS MORE IMPORTANT THAN BEING GOOD

Comic book artist Rob Liefeld (*Deadpool*) isn't the world's greatest artist. In fact, a whole lot of people like to make fun of him for design quirks he can't seem to stop doing, such as obscuring the feet of his characters, covering everyone in weird grimace lines, and adding way too many dang pouches.

---

* "Beefcake" refers to sexy dude art—though in beefcake art there tends to be more of an emphasis on big muscles and powerful bodies, so it's not a one-to-one comparison.

And yet in the nineties, when fax machines roamed wild across the plains of the Serengeti, he was one of the hottest artists in the comic book industry and still gets plenty of work to this day. Why? Because by all accounts he's a professional, dependable guy.

The takeaway here isn't that you should lean into your artistic quirks, refuse to improve, and hope you end up marketable anyway; the takeaway is to be someone audiences and other content creators can depend on. An amazing artist who constantly turns things in late is not someone people will want to collaborate with again, and audiences aren't likely to continue visiting your page if you allow it to lie fallow for weeks and months at a time. Meet your deadlines and keep on posting, even if it's no more than sketches and works-in-progress.

WORDS FROM WORKING NERDS

Hyunsung "Creees" Lee, comic artist/illustrator*

I was always interested in drawing and did it as a hobby, but it was during junior year of high school when I decided to pursue art as a career. After graduating from SVA—the School of Visual Arts—I went straight into drawing comics and going to comic conventions.

Describe an average workday for you.

My average day consists mostly of me live-streaming my work on Twitch.tv. I usually do commissioned illustrations and comic work on there for about six hours. After that, I might spend a couple hours doing studies and other work-related things.

What was your first paid, professionally nerdy project?

Working for Sesame Workshop. During my short time there, I designed some characters and created storyboards for minor projects.

* Creees contributed the illustrations for this book!

What tool could you not do without in your job?

The brush. I really fell in love with brush and ink in my senior year of college. Klaus Janson, a legendary inker at DC Comics (also my professor during my sophomore year at SVA), is the one who told me to try inking with a brush, and now I can't draw without it.

In addition to being a professional artist, you also stream your work. What do you feel are the advantages of pursuing your passions from more than one angle as opposed to putting all your efforts into a single avenue?

Streaming and using social media has allowed me to reach many different types of viewers who I might not have been able to reach without these platforms. For anybody trying to pursue art, I think using social media is super important, [as well as] being consistent with posting.

What tips might you have for newcomers to your field?

I found that drawing popular things such as superheroes and staying on the hype of upcoming things helps people find your work more than just doing your own original work. Don't give up, and work as hard as you can!

SELLING ART IN PERSON: GALLERIES

Presenting and selling your work through galleries and art shows is about as close to "typical" as an artist can have for their career; it's a proud artistic tradition stretching back for centuries. You can make a nice living at it, but it's something heavily limited by geographic availability. If you live in a rural area, odds are low that you'll be able to sustain yourself through gallery sales.

Even if you do live somewhere with some art galleries, making sales at such locations requires serious showmanship skills. A mediocre artist who knows how to monitor trends and sell themselves well will do significantly better than a great artist who ignores trends and is too shy or detached to market themselves. Presence in local galleries will also do little to help your online career, unless you present your online presence aggressively and flamboyantly.

All in all, galleries are a bit of an old person's game at the moment. Often they're run by older folks and stocked with the sort of art that older, well-off people like to put in their homes—art that is rarely of the nerdy persuasion. Twenty, ten—hell, even five years from now, the gallery world may be completely different, so it's worth keeping an eye on even if it's not your main area of interest.

SELLING ART IN PERSON: FAN CONVENTIONS

Many nerdy artists find it easier to sell their work at cons because they're among their people. Trying to explain to a random retired couple from Ohio why they should spend $800 on your Mona Lisa–styled Cersei Lannister portrait is likely to be a losing battle from the start. At a fan convention, you won't have to explain such awesomeness because your fellow nerds will know exactly why your art is awesome.

In addition to heeding the convention tips covered in chapter four, as an artist you'll need a means of transporting your goods. You'll also need said goods. The cost of printing services to create copies of your art will add up quickly; buying a high-quality printer early on and printing your work yourself will save you beaucoup buckos in the long run.

If you're comfortable doing quick work at a convention, taking commissions there can net a strong influx of cash. Plan ahead to give yourself plenty of time to get finished, get paid up-front, and do not haggle or let your customers devalue your art (hard as that may be).

THE PRICE OF PAIN, THE PAIN OF THE PRICE: WHAT TO CHARGE FOR ART?

"An artist is not paid for his labor, but his vision."

—James Whistler

"Darthfield_The_Cat only charges $5 for a black-and-white drawing!" says one potential customer. "Yes," you try to explain, "but they do quick MS Paint sketches and I do graphite work with full gradients." You quickly decide not to say it, fearing it would fall on deaf ears. With a sigh, you lower your price to five dollars even though the work is going to take you upward of four hours. Money is money, right?

Work ethic is great; any kind of nerdy living will be heavily influenced by how much you're willing to push yourself. With that in mind, you can't undervalue yourself as an artist, despite the fact that you'll be fighting against a tide of people trying to get you to do so. "But isn't drawing fun?" they'll say. "You shouldn't be charging at all if you're doing something for fun." While, yeah, art is fun, art is also work that takes time to perform and thousands of hours of practice to master.

No matter what your creative medium, as someone who will spend the bulk of their time self-employed, you're the ultimate judge of what your prices should be.

DON'T PRICE YOUR ART BASED ON WHAT OTHERS ARE DOING

Some artists charge exorbitant amounts for their art because they've accrued the skills, experience, and following that affords them such luxury; there's a reason it would cost a lot more to hire the Beatles to play at your birthday than it would to hire a Beatles cover band.*

Most younger artists will undercut the hell out of themselves in the hopes of making something, *anything* off their work. Price your art based on what you feel is the right price, not because rival artist Darthfield_The_Cat lists their prices a particular way.

---

* Several of the Beatles are dead, for one thing, so there's the added cost of necromancy or time machine rental.

REMEMBER WHAT THE MINIMUM WAGE IS

If you take an $8 commission that takes you six hours to complete, you're working for *way* less than what you'd earn flipping burgers or castrating pigs. Even the most unskilled, entry-level, I-don't-give-a-bat's-butt-about-this-job-but-I-need-the-money positions have a minimum level of pay for employees. Figure out how long it will take to complete a piece, multiply that by at least minimum wage, then round up because most artists undervalue themselves and you probably will, too.

INCLUDE THE PRICE OF MATERIALS IN THE COST

Making art requires supplies: pens, pencils, digital tablets, human blood, quills made from rat spines and raven feathers, all that sort of thing. Price your work with that in mind.

DON'T WORRY THAT SOME PEOPLE WON'T BE ABLE TO AFFORD YOUR ART

No matter what you price your art, there will always be people who want it for cheaper. It's okay that there will be people who can't afford your art; if they like it well enough, they'll remember it and pay for it when they can afford it.

BY UNDERVALUING YOUR ART, YOU ENCOURAGE OTHERS TO DO THE SAME

If you go to an electronics store and see a computer on sale for eighty bucks, odds are high that you're going to wonder what's wrong with it. The same principle applies to art—if you don't present your art as being valuable, no one will value it.

Change your prices with the ebb and flow of supply, demand, and your ever-increasing experience. If more and more people want art from you, obviously you are doing something right and should charge more because—and this is important—your art is *unique*. No one else can create your art the way you do; no one else has your vision.

The same thing goes for experience. When you increase your prices over the years, you're not just doing it to adjust for inflated cost of living (though that's part of it, too). You're doing it because the commissioner is paying for the time spent creating *and* the time spent studying. As your skills increase, so, too, should your prices.

NEVER GET DEFENSIVE ABOUT COST

Your prices are the way they are; don't let potential customers' complaints ("B-but Darthfield doesn't charge so much!") make you feel as if you should lower prices. By trying to defend yourself, it makes you sound weaker to the customer and *feel* weaker, increasing the likelihood you'll do the same work for less than you deserve. When discussing pricing, remember this simple statement: "These are my prices. If you don't like them, you can buy someone else's art."

IF YOU FEEL LIKE YOU'RE BEING TAKEN ADVANTAGE OF, YOU ARE

If you resent your customers, if you feel like they're just buying your art because you don't charge enough for it, it's time to make a change. Raise your prices, take fewer commissions, and don't let people push you around as much with their demands.

SOMETIMES THE MONEY ISN'T WORTH IT

Maybe you have a customer willing to pay a ton for a piece, but you feel uncomfortable with the intent behind it, like maybe you get the feeling the art they want is a not-so-subtle smear piece against an ex they feel wronged by. Maybe the customer is way too specific and the work would be a pain in the ass because you'd have to tweak it repeatedly. Maybe it's too icky. Whatever your reason, if your spidey-sense is tingling that the customer will be too much of a hassle to work with, don't do it. The amount of time, effort, and mental energy expended on this one pain-in-the-ass customer could cause you to miss out on other, better opportunities.

To be an artist—a creator—means to summon something from nothing, to find meaning in madness, to express yourself without knowing that your meaning will be interpreted as you intended. While this is true for all types of creators, it is, perhaps, most true for the creators whose works reside primarily in the imagination: authors.

CHAPTER NINE

WRITING BOOKS

O f the many nerdy pursuits, publishing is still among the most arcane in its path to success, requiring would-be novelists to tame the strange, dark beast known as the publishing industry.

Being a writer in the twenty-first century is vastly different than it was in centuries past. Today's writers have to worry about online ratings, word of mouth, social media presence, review bombs, and probably other weird Internet-related things that haven't been invented yet, all adding up to a pile of extra headaches and social complications. Conversely, there are more opportunities to pursue your dreams than ever before; while decades past saw novelists at the mercy of a few all-powerful gatekeepers, today it's easier than ever for raw determination to win out in the face of adversity.

Now, before you worry about sending out review copies of your book to market-friendly sites, before you ply your parents for some five-star ratings, before you ever fret about how to go about your first AMA, there's something much more pressing you need to do with your book—write the sucker.

STARTING POINT: WRITING

There are pa-*lenty* of books out there devoted to teaching you how to build a career as an author. This book is about teaching you how to build a career as a nerd, and this chapter specifically is about building a career as a nerdy author. As with all things, wordsmithing continues to evolve alongside the Internet, and the modern writer needs to evolve alongside it.

PUNCH THE KEYS, FOR GOD'S SAKE: DELETING PROCRASTINATION

Writers read, and writers write. Writing, however, requires a certain amount of willpower to even begin. Posting online videos, streaming, etc., have built-in pressures to keep you on track because if you don't stay active you're likely to lose some of your accumulated audience and draw the ire of a horde of irritable commenters. When you're first starting as a writer, the only person you have to be accountable to is you. Sure, once you've got a literary agent and a publishing house breathing down your neck to get the manuscript done, you'll feel the heat, but there's a large distance between here and there, and the only way to cover that distance is through self-motivation. This means finding your sources of procrastination and beating them until they're bloody and broken in an alley.

Ignore the temptations of the online world. Checking Facebook, rummaging through Twitter, browsing your favorite clown-hunting sites . . . these are all things that can wait until *after* you've knocked out your target word count. Make a hard rule to ignore the Internet until you've accomplished your goals for the day. There are programs and apps such as ColdTurkeyBlocker that force you to get to work until you've hit your goal. So if you don't want to risk temptation, find a program that will use its cold computer logic to prevent you from getting distracted.

Commit publicly, because peer pressure *works*. If you're accountable to other human beings who will be checking up on your progress, you'll be less likely to foofoo* around.

Use a to-do list if you're prone to disorganization. Organize your list to prioritize which tasks are critical and which can be done last. Set up reminders in your phone for deadlines and such so your present self can watch your future self's back.

Move around. Light exercise can help get you going if you're stuck on what to write.

Don't strive for perfection, strive for accomplishment. A lot of would-be writers I've talked to say they've got such perfectionist tendencies that they

---

* What? That's a real word. Don't go looking it up!

can't let themselves write less-than-perfect material. News flash: Even the greatest writers in history don't perfectly crush their first drafts between their muscular buttocks. By performing the sheer task of writing, no matter whether you're filling every page with mind-expanding perfection or utter drivel, you're still doing better than the people who write nothing because at least you've created *something*. Plus, bad writing can become good writing either through editing or by serving as a lesson on what not to write in the future. If you have a tendency toward the need for perfection, channel it into a need to hit a perfect word count for the day or to write for the perfect amount of time. Whatever your method is, just write, damn you, write!

Everyone procrastinates. Every professional has days when they stare at a blank screen and decide to clean their keyboard instead of getting any major work done. The difference between them and a wannabe writer is wannabes sit around thinking about writing without ever even firing up their word processor. Real writers know getting past procrastination can be as simple as turning on the computer and focusing for a half hour every day to get some words thrown at the page.

THE NEVER-ENDING HUNT FOR IDEAS

Ah, great! You've got a day free to write, you're sitting at your keyboard, and you've got delicious coffee sitting all warm and toasty in your Darth Vader mug. Time to write!

. . . Except the only idea you have is fanfiction of Optimus Prime teaming up with the trucker chimpanzee from *B. J. and the Bear* to travel across America solving crimes. Gotta find some inspiration!

Story ideas can come from nearly anywhere. They do not, as a rule, come from repetition. If you're doing the same things every day—watching the same shows, visiting the same places, talking to the same people—you're limiting your potential for finding new story ideas. If you want to find a new idea for a book, broaden your horizons a bit. Go to a museum. Hang out at a new coffeeshop and eavesdrop (in an artist-searching-for-inspiration way, not in a creepy-weirdo-listening-too-intently-to-strangers kind of way). Browse outside of your usual websites. Talk to people who work at the county fair. Go to a sporting event. Do *something* out of the ordinary. Even if you don't find the core element of your next book, you'll probably find some worthwhile nuggets of humanity worth writing down and examining further.

Think about something you're fascinated by, whether it's a historical event, a location, a person, a phenomenon, a mythological creature, or something else altogether. Find ways to reimagine the object of your fascination to see what sorts of stories might arise. *World War II But the Nazis Are Terminators*; *The Care Bears But They're Government Assassins On the Side*; *The Brady Bunch But They're Secretly Aliens*. Sometimes greatness can come from taking something utterly familiar and giving it the smallest twist.

Find writing prompts and do them. Some writers scoff at the idea of using writing prompts to come up with story hooks; the rest of us call them pretentious goobers. Writing prompts can be great ways to uncover your next big story idea, or, at the very least, give you a decent exercise in creative thinking. If you're stuck for some prompts, here are a few you can have:

- A parent wakes up convinced their kids have been replaced, but no one else sees it.

- A teenager discovers they have the ability to enter other people's minds and steal their talents, fears, and desires.

- A promising young scientist invents a time machine and receives a note from themselves in the future saying to destroy the machine.

- A disillusioned former spy gets called back in by the organization they abandoned. The mission? Take down the spy who taught them everything they know.

- A man has a simple goal: Eat a sandwich on his birthday.

Another way to get a story idea is to take the concept of one story and reverse it. For example, let's try reversing the sample prompts above:

- Two kid siblings wake up convinced their parents have been replaced, but no one else sees it.

- A teenager discovers they have the power to let others enter their mind and lend out their talents, fears, and desires.

- A washed-up scientist gets a mysterious note in their own handwriting; it's a blueprint to build a time machine, with an invitation to come join them in the future once it's finished.

- A disillusioned former spy gets called back by the master who taught them everything they know. The mission? Take down the organization they abandoned.

- A sandwich has a simple goal: Eat a man on his birthday.

Smash together two disparate story ideas, otherwise referred to as "start with the hook." The quickest, easiest way to hook people with your story idea is to use existing stories people are already familiar with. "It's like *Dragon Ball Z* meets *Vampire Hunter D*!" "It's like *Metal Gear Solid* meets *Gilligan's Island*!" "It's like *The X-Files* meets *Golden Girls* with a little bit of Tyler Perry's *Boo 2!: A Madea Halloween*!" Start smashing together previous works to see what you can make out of it.

Follow your curiosity. If something grabs your attention, follow it. Research it. Learn everything you can about it. You never know what might end up inspiring your next work . . . so long as you don't go so deep down the rabbit hole that you never end up starting/working on/completing that work.

Don't worry about someone stealing your idea. Here's another mistake I see newbies make—they're so afraid of someone else stealing their idea that they refuse to let anyone see it (though I'm sure this secrecy also stems from a fear that someone else will give a critique they don't like). An unknowable number of stories exist already; the likelihood that you're going to create a compelling story that's 100-percent unique is 0 percent.

There's an old, cynical writer's adage that states "There are no new ideas." That's true, from a certain point of view, yet entirely false. Consider this: If J. K. Rowling and Stephen King both tell a story about a little boy who discovers a magical being in his basement, those two stories are going to be *very* different. A story isn't about the core concept; it's about the execution of that concept. *My Hero Academia* is kind of *Heroes*, which is basically *s-CRY-ed*, which is sort of *The Tomorrow People*, which is more or less *X-Men*. All of these stories have powerful similarities, and yet they're entirely dissimilar because their themes, their characters, their *execution* is different. Don't worry about someone else stealing your perfect story idea; worry about taking that perfect idea and instilling your voice perfectly into it.

Mine your past, but don't strip-mine your past. Using pieces of your personal history for inspiration is an excellent idea. What you should probably not do, however, is write a no-holds-barred more-or-less-true novel about your life. While many interesting things have probably happened to you, it's unlikely your life story will make for a good book unless your name happens to be Malala Yousafzai. Mine your past for useful story nuggets and take those nuggets to refine into something greater in your fiction.*

---

* Also, people can get weirdly litigious when writers include them (or thinly veiled versions of them) in their work. If you stick to writing fiction, you're probably fine. If you're writing an autobiography, however, there's the potential for some sticky legal issues down the road.

WORDS FROM WORKING NERDS

Bethany Claire is best known for writing the *USA Today*-bestselling Morna's Legacy series. Bethany is also cofounder of MasteringSelfPublishing.com, a site dedicated to helping writers by providing online courses and resources for their self-publishing journey.

I started writing creatively in college. It was my outlet, something I did to relieve stress and distract myself from the fact that I was working toward a major I truly had no passion for. I was an elementary education major, and, while I love children and think teachers have one of the most important jobs in the world, I knew deep down I wasn't supposed to be a teacher. The more time I spent writing, the more I knew I wanted to write full-time. Finally, while I was sitting in a summer session education-methods class—my last class before my semester of student teaching and graduation—I had a moment of total clarity. I quietly gathered my things, left the classroom, and walked down to the registrar's office, where I withdrew from the university on the spot. I then threw myself into learning everything I could about publishing—both traditional and self-publishing—and quickly decided self-publishing was the only side of publishing I had any interest in. I worked nonstop for the next five months, learning, writing, and preparing for the launch of the first three books in my series. I launched them in November 2013. Within six months, the series landed on the *USA Today* bestseller list, and I've been writing full-time ever since.

What has surprised you the most about online publishing?

I think the most surprising thing has been discovering how much is possible if you stay constantly on the lookout for new things. If you continue to keep up to date on how the industry is always changing, the possibilities really are limitless.

What obstacles do you feel are in the way for self-published authors?

I think the biggest obstacle for me was overcoming other people's judgments and opinions. So many people tried to talk me out of doing this. Only my closest family members believed in me enough to think self-publishing was a good idea. I'm quite sure a lot of people thought I'd completely lost my mind when they learned I'd dropped out of college so close to graduation, but it was honestly the best decision I've ever made. It kept me from having a backup plan, and I think that was a huge reason why I succeeded. I didn't allow myself any other option.

What do you feel are the advantages and disadvantages of online publishing, as opposed to traditional publishing?

Honestly, I think it all boils down to one thing . . . control. When self-publishing, you control your own destiny. You control your covers, your pricing, when you run sales, and how you market your books. You also get to keep so much more of your profit.

If you're someone who wants to write and you're not interested in the publishing side of things—the marketing or the preparation, etc.—then self-publishing is definitely not for you and traditional publishing would hold more advantages, but that's one of the only circumstances where I believe self-publishing has a disadvantage to traditional publishing. If you do it right, it's way more work, because you are doing every part of the publishing process yourself.

What should a writer know before getting involved in self-publishing?

First: Educate yourself. Read, take courses, go to conferences—do everything you can to learn the business. Second: Always put writing first. There's no business to promote or grow without the books. Your craft should always be your top priority. Third: Hire professionals. Never create your own cover or do your own editing. Hire people who know what they're doing and are experts in their field. It's worth the investment and can make a huge difference in whether or not your books succeed.

What do you feel are the advantages of using a nom de plume?

There are lots of reasons someone might choose to write under a pen name (I do!). Someone may want to disguise their gender—i.e., a male who writes romance or a female who is writing in a very male-dominated genre. Or someone's name may be too long to look good on a cover, or perhaps it's too hard to pronounce or isn't catchy enough. The biggest advantage in my opinion, though, is that it really has helped me create a clear separation between my professional and personal lives, which I enjoy.

BUILDING CHARACTERS

Characters, the *dramatis personae*, are those little fictional people we create to use as fabric in the grand tapestry of our narrative. While there are a near-infinite number of fictional characters, each with their own little human details, as writers we must consider them both in the personal and impersonal sense, considering their thoughts and feelings as sentient beings while also planning how they best weave into the story. In regards to characters-as-story-components, there are a few distinct types every writer should know:*

The **protagonist** is the character you're supposed to root for, the "hero." The protagonist is usually going to be the character with the most pronounced character arc, meaning they will be the most changed by story's end.

To be clear, just because someone is your story's hero doesn't mean they're going to be heroic, necessarily. Walter White from *Breaking Bad* and Light Yagami from *Death Note* are the "hero" of each of their stories but are also a couple of very bad boys whose stories make it clear that their flaws are to be learned from, not admired.

A protagonist must be sympathetic in that they are understandable. We may not know what it's like to have the weight of an empire on our shoulders or an insatiable lust for human blood, but we need to understand the core human emotions behind such fantastic problems.

In Blake Snyder's *Save the Cat!*, he describes numerous examples of characters who, despite being dislikable or potentially evil on paper, hold our interest. These characters grab us thanks to a combination of charm, intrigue, and the utilization of a **Save the Cat** moment—a critical moment early in the story that reveals a human, empathetic element to the protagonist that makes the audience connect with them. This can be accomplished many ways—a quick exchange of witty yet heartfelt dialogue, your character standing up for someone more downtrodden than they are, saving a literal cat, etc.

Secondary characters exist to further the themes of your story, to act as help or hindrance to your protagonist, to define your setting, and to keep the

---

* There will be some of you out there tempted to point out the ways in which you feel these writing rules, tips, and techniques are wrong, citing the work of your favorite authors. Again, let me say what I said wayyyy back in the blogging chapter: One must learn the rules to know when it's okay to break them.

plot moving. Secondary characters need relatively uncomplicated backstories to prevent the reader from getting confused—and you from wasting your time on utterly unnecessary details.

Many secondary characters are actually **foils** whose purpose is to magnify or reflect the existing traits of a more prominent character by comparison. Sherlock Holmes's partner and assistant, Watson, is the archetypal example of a foil, as he often stood around remarking how clever the legendary detective was. The "best friends" in any romantic comedy are generally foils, with the sloppy, gross male best friend making the male lead seem more together, and the promiscuous female best friend making the female lead seem more desirable. Foils are strong character tools but must be used sparingly lest they become annoying and obvious.

Tertiary characters are only around for an instant. They're there to further the theme a tiny bit, or to flesh out your world to make it feel real, or to be weird, outrageous, and hilarious, infusing some hot sauce into a scene that's otherwise a bit too original-recipe. Hannibal Chau from *Pacific Rim*, the Sommelier from *John Wick: Chapter 2*, or Koh the Face Stealer from *Avatar: The Last Airbender* are all fantastic tertiary characters, staying around just long enough to spark our interest and expand their fictional worlds.

For every action, there is an equal but opposite reaction. For every main character, there must be an equal but opposite force pushing against them. That's the **antagonist.** The antagonist reflects our hero and opposes their journey toward self-actualization.

The antagonist wants to prevent the hero from getting that which they desire most. They're usually static characters, foiled by their inability to change, providing a sharp contrast to the (usually) dynamic growth of the protagonist. Antagonists often justify their behaviors through their own warped sense of morality, and, much as a protagonist doesn't have to be heroic, an antagonist doesn't have to be villainous to serve that purpose in the story. *The Fugitive*'s US Marshal Sam Gerard is an officer on the right side of the law, chasing down our hero for a crime he didn't commit and serving as that film's antagonist. In *Captain America: Civil War*, Cap and Iron Man both act as protagonists and each other's antagonist.

With antagonists, the key to writing them is to realize that they wouldn't consider themselves antagonists. Dracula probably didn't wake up every evening, look at his stupid little slicked-back hairdo in the mirror, and think, *Yep, I'm such a supervillain that people will be writing stories with me as the antagonist for centuries to come.*[*] Many villains consider what they do to be a necessary evil in the pursuit of higher goals. As a writer, it's up to you to figure out what it is about these baddies that is human enough for an audience to find interest in.

With any character, no matter their purpose in your story, try to figure out whether that specific character is necessary or if they could be combined with another underused character to simplify and streamline things.

Don't be too precious with any of them; your characters are there in service of the story, so don't make them oh-so-perfect little Mary Sues; torture them when need be. Make them flawed and make them *hurt* and you'll be on the right track to a story worth telling.

CRAFTING PLOT

In *The Seven Basic Plots: Why We Tell Stories*, author Christopher Booker posits that all stories can be divided into seven broad categories. Many writers disagree with this idea, as broadly categorizing disparate stories together based on general rules isn't as elucidating as you might expect. *Frankenstein*, *Shrek*, and *JoJo's Bizarre Adventure*, for example, would all fall under the same type of story despite being about as different as stories can be.[†] However, breaking stories down into their elemental components does serve as a useful way of examining them, thinking about them, re-contextualizing them. Take a look at the stories you love the most, try to find the parallels between them, and use that as a stepping-off point for your own works.

THE BIG G: GENRE

Some writers rebel against the idea of "genre" by creating wild, genre-straddling works that push the envelope of story structure; most stories, however, fall into broad categories based on the primary intent of the tale.

---

[*] He didn't think that for many reasons, not the least of which is vampires don't cast reflections.

[†] Though a team-up between the three franchises would be hella awesome.

The genre you choose is up to you, and the first step toward figuring out what genre to write is to examine what you read. If you read a lot of gritty, realistic crime novels, you're probably not going to write much epic fantasy. We write what we read, and we should *want* to read the stories we're writing.

HORROR

Stories that turn a mirror on society's darkest impulses to garner understanding of ourselves, often incorporating fantastic elements as metaphors for our most terrible thoughts. Horror stories are generally meant to disgust and terrify readers, as both a way of increasing understanding and of allowing us to experience and control our fears.

> ♦ **Examples:** *The Shining, It, Dracula, House of Leaves*

SCIENCE FICTION

Stories that provide projective critiques of current and future society through the use of not-quite-real technology. Sci-fi stories generally avoid the supernatural, even if the science is loosey-goosey at best, often covering hypothetical scientific topics such as extraterrestrial life, time travel, parallel dimensions, and Martha Stewart.

> ♦ **Examples:** *Frankenstein, Fahrenheit 451, Ringworld*

FANTASY

Stories that focus on providing a fantastic setting to inspire the reader's imagination and provide them an escape from the mundane, even unpleasant, world around them. Fantasy stories are often about building a grand mythology in which the reader can get lost, rewarding those who lose themselves in the details of these rich worlds.

> ♦ **Examples:** the Harry Potter series, the Lord of the Rings series, the
> Game of Thrones series, the Discworld series

YOUNG ADULT

Stories with themes of transformation and discovery of identity, framed around the perspective of an adolescent hero. Young adult (YA) is a broad genre that combines well with others, which is why the YA sections of most bookstores and libraries are subdivided based on subgenres such as YA fantasy, YA drama, YA romance, and even YA paranormal romance (you can thank *Twilight* for that one).

> ◆ **Examples:** the Hunger Games series, *The Fault in Our Stars*, *The Outsiders*

MYSTERY

Stories designed to titillate the logic of the reader and to create a grand game in which the reader can take part.

> ◆ **Examples:** *Presumed Innocent*, *The Maltese Falcon*, everything Sherlock Holmes

ROMANCE

Stories designed to stir the emotions, resolving in a satisfying and optimistic finale.*

> ◆ **Examples:** *Pride and Prejudice*, *Jane Eyre*, *Outlander*

THRILLER

Stories designed to deliver thrills and keep the audience's tense little booties right at the edge of their seats. Thrillers mostly shy away from supernatural elements, embracing the real world over a fantasy world.

> ◆ **Examples:** Most of the works of Dan Brown, James Patterson, Tom Clancy; basically, if you can buy it at an airport, it's probably a thriller

---

* Unless it's a tragic romance, aka a Nicholas Sparks novel, in which case somebody gon' die.

DRAMA

Stories that use fictional people in realistic settings to illuminate real feelings, ideas, and problems.

- **Examples:** *The Kite Runner, Memoirs of a Geisha, The Book Thief*

NONFICTION

Stories of real events and real people, filtered through the imagination of a writer to organize it in a way that gives these past events present meaning. Should this be your choice of genre, prepare for lots of research in your future.*

- **Examples:** *The Immortal Life of Henrietta Lacks, Into the Wild, March, My Friend Dahmer, The Story of My Tits*

IF YOU BUILD IT, THEY WILL READ: STORY STRUCTURE

While there are many ways to piece together fiction, most stories for Western audiences adhere to a singular adaptive pattern. In Joseph Campbell's *The Hero with a Thousand Faces,* Campbell analyzes story patterns and Jungian archetypes to define this structure as the *monomyth,* a singular story structure around which most stories are built. George Lucas made good use of the monomyth in his creation of *Star Wars,* which is one of the many reasons *A New Hope* became the universal hit it is.

The monomythic story begins with the **ordinary world**, a portion of the story that establishes the stakes, characters, and setting of your tale.

- *Star Wars* **Example:** Farm boy Luke hungers for adventure outside of his dull life on Tatooine.

---

* And prepare for a potentially easier path to income, as nonfiction books can sometimes be sold based on a solid query letter, proposal, and credentials, unlike fiction, where you'll almost always have to have a completed novel before you can begin shopping it around.

The **call to adventure** is the inciting incident that kicks your story off by forcing your protagonist to make a choice that could result in change.

- ◆ *Star Wars* **Example:** Luke finds the secret message in R2-D2.

The **refusal of the call** is when the protagonist weighs the costs/benefits of the journey they may face.

- ◆ *Star Wars* **Example:** Luke goes after R2-D2, but doesn't commit to joining the rebellion.

Meeting the mentor is when our hero meets the wise mofo who's gonna dispense wisdomous advice.

- ◆ *Star Wars* **Example:** Luke meets Ben Kenobi, who teaches him a bit about the Force.

Crossing the threshold is where our hero crosses over into an unknown world.

- ◆ *Star Wars* **Example:** Luke and Ben head into the Mos Eisley cantina, a world unlike anything Luke knows.

Tests, allies, and enemies present the moment when our hero faces their first real challenges, meets some allies, and also meets some not-so-allies.

- ◆ *Star Wars* **Example:** Luke meets Han and Chewie, and they have to escape Imperial soldiers.

Approach to the innermost cave is when the stakes are established and the story's players move in for a massive conflict.

- ◆ *Star Wars* **Example:** Luke learns more about the Force as the group heads to Alderaan and finds it's done been blowed up real good.

The **ordeal** is when our hero undergoes their most strenuous trial yet. If the hero fails, all their struggles will have been for nothing and everything they hold dear will be lost. The hero's victory often comes at deep cost.

- ◆ *Star Wars* **Example:** Luke and the gang rescue Leia, but Ben loses his battle with Darth Vader and becomes one with the Force.

The **moment of reward** is where our hero obtains the lesson or object they need to triumph.

- ◆ *Star Wars* **Example:** Luke joins the Rebellion, just as he wanted to way back at the beginning of Act I.

The **road back** is the moment when the hero has to decide between adhering to their old way of thinking or abandoning it entirely to grow as a person.

- ◆ *Star Wars* **Example:** Luke can either make the selfish choice to leave with Han or the selfless, dangerous choice to stay with the Rebellion.

Resurrection takes place when our hero faces their toughest trial yet, emerging from the challenge reborn as someone new.

- ◆ *Star Wars* **Example:** Luke embraces his path as a Jedi to destroy the Death Star.

Then comes the **return with the elixir**, wherein our hero returns, rewarded and transformed, to their previous life.

- ◆ *Star Wars* **Example:** Luke doesn't go back to Tatooine here, instead finding himself a changed man who is rewarded for his efforts by becoming part of a larger universe.

Some argue that following such a template too closely can result in stale storytelling. Blake Snyder's *Save the Cat!*, for example, has a wonderful little beat sheet that outlines the monomyth in Hollywood script-friendly beats but has also resulted in numerous writers adhering so closely to the beat sheet that their stories become formulaic. Even *Star Wars: A New Hope*, which is about as formulaic as you could ever expect to find, deviates a bit from the formula at certain points. Regardless of how you choose to structure your story, it's important that you understand these common story beats so you know how to build/mislead the expectations of your audience.

REFINING PROSE

Strong characters and plot are the guts and nerves of a good story, but you want it to have some flowing hair and soft skin to go along with those gooey internal organs, and, in this increasingly yucky metaphor, that's going to be your prose.

Prose refers to language unbound by metrical structure—i.e., not poetry. Writers often use prose to refer to everything—dialogue, characters, descriptions, emotions, environments, etc. Many new writers will make the mistake of crafting prose that is more functional than emotive; they'll describe a room, the people in it, and what they are saying without taking a moment to ornament their words with the richness of metaphors.

> The room was big and black and made Lancie feel cold. Its walls were flat and not very pretty.
>
> *Brr*, thought Lancie. *I'm cold.*
>
> "Hey," Tyban, who looked tired, said to Lancie.
>
> "Hey," she sadly replied. "I didn't find anything about those vampires, which is bad."

You'll notice that the sheet of paper this page is on is 11 percent softer than the rest of the book. That's because I knew you would fall asleep while reading that snore-fest of a section and wanted to give you somewhere nice to rest your head.

Newbie writers are often so concerned with the act of getting their story assembled that they build what it essentially a screenplay, only bothering to denote character names, actions, and backgrounds the with barest of unornamented description. This sort of writing flows like a water fountain with someone's thumb over it, sputtering, spewing, and spilling everywhere in a way which satisfies no one. For prose to truly flow, it needs emotion. It needs the colorful, wonderful thing we call *metaphor*. It needs to go beyond merely telling what's happening— it needs to *show* it.

> Every sound, no matter how minute, echoed along the unornamented walls of the Obsidian Room. Lancie suppressed a shiver as she stepped through the open archway.
>
> Tyban leaned against a table covered with maps and notes and the little figurines he claimed helped him plan military strategies but were mostly there because he liked the look of them. Deep, purple grooves marred the skin beneath his eyes, as if his worries had spent the night pacing back and forth across his face. His lips were cracked, his beard unkempt.
>
> It took him a moment to notice Lancie; he quirked a brow at her without a word.
>
> She sighed and shook her head no.

While I'm certainly not claiming that the above section is the World's Most Perfectest Prose Ever Written, I feel confident in proclaiming it to be better than the prose that preceded it. It's a section that *shows*—rather than *tells*—you what the characters are feeling.

STARTING POINT: TRADITIONAL PUBLISHING

The publishing landscape spent most of its years fairly solidified. As with most industries, however, the advent of the Internet has thrown publishers for a loop. While the additional opportunities for connections afforded to you by the Internet are undoubtedly a good thing, with these opportunities come additional responsibilities that you, dear writer, will need to understand and undertake.

HAVING A SOCIAL MEDIA PRESENCE HELPS, BUT IT ISN'T REQUIRED

If you're publishing traditionally these days, you can get away with being an offline recluse. Your literary agent will probably put together some kind of a shell of an online presence, like a minimalist Twitter account that mostly tweets publishing dates, interviews with you, and articles featuring your work. You'll probably get strongly encouraged to get online, and, given that you're reading this book, you probably already *are* online, so you might as well make the most of it.

DON'T READ THE REVIEWS

When your book comes out, it's very tempting to read every review of it. Don't.

For the love of Thor, *don't* read the reviews, no matter whether they're professionals doing full write-up reviews or quick Amazon reviews. We humans have a quirk called the **negativity bias**, which is the tendency to pay better attention to, and remember, negative information than positive information. While from an evolutionary perspective this has helped us become better at deciphering dangerous situations, it also has the unpleasant side effect of making us retain negative memories more strongly than the positive. Magician Penn Jillette, on an episode of the *Nerdist* podcast, recounted how he'd had numerous positive interactions on Twitter with people telling him they'd enjoyed his work, and yet the messages he remembered most were when people were being jerks.[28] Of all the reviews of my books, one that has stuck with me over the years was from a random goober who complained about my writing using a pile of grammar so abhorrent to look at that it was almost Lovecraftian.

The best thing to do with reviews is to ignore them until you can have someone you know, someone you trust, read them when you're not watching them for their every reaction. Let them filter through the reviews more objectively than you can, sifting through the worthwhile critiques and legitimate positive points and angry ramblings. It'll let you keep learning from your mistakes without sticking in your craw quite as hard. Critiques are an important part of building your skill as a writer, but not everyone with an opinion is going to give you a good critique. Bad reviews can be severely discouraging, no matter how far along you are in your career; when you're a newbie writer, however, that discouragement can lead to the abandonment of your career.

PUBLISHING SUCCESS CAN BE ACHIEVED THROUGH SUCCESS IN OTHER FIELDS

If you have a successful-enough blog, YouTube channel, or, hell, even Instagram account, you may end up getting offered a book deal about your topic of choice. Being famous for one thing makes you an enticing property to people who sell *other* things. Just think of how many mouth-breathing celebrities have books (most of which were ghost-written for them by people who know the difference between a colon and a large intestine).

However, tons of terrific, smart people get book deals based on their other works, people such as Felicia Day or even my wife, Katrina "Action Chick" Hill, whose action-movie blog led to her first book deal. The YouTube series *The Haunting of Sunshine Girl* gained such popularity that it spun off into a series of novels based on the work.

If you do something well, don't be surprised if you get a book offer someday. Still, if your heart's goal is to write a book, don't focus exclusively on trying to become a YouTube star in the hopes of getting a book deal. That's a silly use of your time and energy.

GO TO BOOK CONVENTIONS, WRITING CONVENTIONS, ALL KINDS OF CONVENTIONS!

I've espoused the virtues of attending fan conventions elsewhere throughout the book; those benefits apply to professional writers as much as they do any other professionally nerdy career.

Writing-oriented conventions, the kinds with literary agents, publishers, and published authors as the main guests, are an invaluable resource for any up-and-coming writer. Getting face time with agents and the other people in power will help you learn the sorts of things they're looking for, as well as becoming more memorable to them in the future (hopefully for a good reason, not because you were so nervous that you forgot your business cards and spit on yourself and tried unsuccessfully to laugh it all off like I did).

Writing conventions also offer real-time experiences you can't get anywhere else in the form of lectures and workshops. DFWCon, a Dallas-area writing convention, famously has a Gong Show for its writers. The set-up? Writers submit their query letters to a panel of three agents. The letters are then read, aloud, in front of a crowd of hopeful writers and the agents audibly reject the letters the instant they're no longer interested. Sure, it's brutal to see your work potentially get ripped to shreds with people watching, but it's a brutally effective learning tool for seeing where your query needs work, as each literary agent explains *why* they rejected your letter when they did. On the less nerve-wracking side of things, writing conventions also offer classes where professionals will share craft secrets and techniques, Q & A sessions with literary agents and other important literary folks, classes on nitty-gritty technical and financial details you might not think to research because you don't know they exist, and workshops where the pros will help you get past that thing keeping your story stuck in chapter eleven. These are the sorts of experiences you can't get without hitting the convention circuit.

WORDS FROM WORKING NERDS

Regina Richards, award-winning author of gothic historical romance and fantasy adventure with strong romantic elements, such as the gothic *Blood Marriage* and the fantasy-adventure *The Blue Breeze*, the first in the Hell Hollows series

Russ Linton, author of the gritty superhero Crimson Son series—*Crimson Son*, *Motherland*, and the short story collection *Empty Quiver*—and the "Kafka and Tolkien on the Ganges" fantasy series The Stormblade Saga—*Pilgrim of the Storm*, *Forge of the Jadugar*, and *Wake of Alshasra'a*

Annie Neugebauer, author of speculative fiction, literary fiction, poetry, and blog columns, and perhaps most known for horror

Dan Hammond, author of *Delbert Judd*, *The Solomon Twist*, and the short story collection *Ice*

Jennifer August, author of erotic romance novels such as *Affair of Convenience*, *His Lady Thief*, *Knight of the Mist*, and the Sexual Magic series

Lisa Bubert, a writer whose fiction and poetry have appeared in *Carolina Quarterly*, *Wildness*, *Barnstorm Journal*, *Spartan*, and more; her story "Formation" was named a finalist in the Texas Institute of Letters Kay Cattarrula Award for Best Short Story

LANGLEY:

How did you get started as writers?

RICHARDS:

I knew I wanted to write from the moment I held my first book in my hands as a child, but there was no support for that desire from either teachers or parents. They were all certain I should be a lawyer or a politician. But those were their dreams, not mine. Anyway, life kept happening and writing didn't. Though a tremendous amount of reading did!

In 2003, I agreed to teach a class on writing to a group of homeschool students. While doing research for that class, I discovered a community of writers online who were critiquing one another's work. I sat down and wrote something and submitted it for critique. My inbox started to fill surprisingly quickly, but I was afraid to look at the critiques, so I allowed them to pile up for days. When I finally opened and read them, they were glowing beyond my wildest dreams. I laid my head on my desk and cried for joy.

From then on, I began writing and honing my craft. In 2012, I published my first novel to excellent reviews. I truly love this work. My only regret is that I didn't begin sooner.

LINTON:

After college, I bounced around a bit between creative outlets, crazy adventures, and raising my son. In 2012, I decided to enroll in an online creative writing course through Stanford, and the feedback there was encouraging enough that I started submitting stories that year.

When I finished my first novel, *Crimson Son,* in late 2013, I'd been submitting stories to online magazines and anthologies for two years. With half a dozen published stories and articles under my belt, I'd had plenty of practice for the trad pub [traditional publishing] gauntlet to follow. But I'm maybe not known for my patience. I made the decision to self-publish then and haven't looked back.

BUBERT:

I wrote my first poem at age eight. It was about buttercups, and my mom really loved it. My second manifesto was at age nine when I researched my family history in Texas (the obsession started early). I've written off and on, but only really got serious about it after I graduated with my library degree, got married, and found myself without any new items I needed to check off on the to-do list of life. It took me a long time to take myself seriously as a writer; I spent a lot of time waiting for someone else to bestow the title on me, kind of like they do when they hire you as a librarian and then hey! you're a librarian now.

LANGLEY:

Where do you find ideas and inspirations for your writing?

AUGUST:

My critique partners and groups. Critique groups are great for gathering myriad responses to your writing—especially multi-genre groups. A lot of my male characters have been strengthened by critiques from the men in my critique groups because they provide insight into a guy's brain. They give me the unvarnished truth and swift kick in the pants I need, whether it's reworking a piece in the book or pushing me to write.

NEUGEBAUER:

Everywhere and anywhere—isn't that an infuriating answer? But it's true; there's no one source I go to for ideas. I live my life, consume art, think, and ideas manifest as a natural result of my interests, beliefs, and experiences. I might be researching one thing and watching a TV show that sparks a new combination. Or I could be struggling with something in my life and discover that a strange metaphor is the best way to capture that issue in fiction. The possibilities are endless, which is really the most beautiful thing about ideas: There are *always* more. And creativity is a muscle, so the more you come up with ideas, the easier it is to come up with more.

LINTON:

Friends and fellow authors. People exactly like me pursuing their dreams. Writers are an odd bundle of introverted souls with manic interests and exuberant opinions. Chances are, wherever you live, there is a group of like-minded souls on the same path, and I highly recommend seeking them out for advice, inspiration, and butt jokes.

HAMMOND:

Nothing inspires me more than working through plots with other writers or speaking in general about the process. I'm old-school, so I appreciate the dogged, write-everyday efforts of John Updike. I appreciate the passion for writing that Frank Conroy expressed.

LANGLEY:

What tips do you have for defeating procrastination and other obstacles as a writer?

LINTON:

There are a whole slew of mental obstacles to overcome as a writer. "Am I good enough? Will anyone read what I've written? How can I write another word on this damn book?" There are stigmas about self-publishers, impossible economic realities of an overcrowded industry, and relentless politics infiltrating even creative pursuits. Like most obstacles, you tear them down through plain old mental toughness.

Many people, however, face obstacles that they simply can't think their way past or get tough about. As a writer, I do have my own bundle of quirks and issues that could possibly be described on some clinical scale. (I don't think I'm overstepping by saying this is a common thing among creative types.) But I've learned to understand these to be not just obstacles but part of who I am, which informs my creative process.

You have to feel deeply driven to write to make the effort and emotional expense worth it. It's hard. I've been doing this for ten years, and it's still so *hard*. If anything, it has only gotten more difficult. I imagine a lot of people start, realize the effort outweighs the benefits for them, and move on. I think that's fine. No shame in not wanting to dedicate your life to such a specific and finicky pursuit. But if it's what you want, you have to be willing to work through all the barriers and setbacks.

Ira Glass captures another reason many would-be writers quit: the gap between our taste and our abilities. If you're an avid reader, as most writers are, you've probably developed fantastic taste. You know when a book is high quality, well written, beautifully paced, etc. But when you decide to write one of your own, it won't be. Writing is a highly nuanced combination of skills that takes years to master; *of course* you don't start out awesome at it. That's frustrating and disappointing—to know what you want to create but not yet be capable of doing it. So a lot of writers quit, assuming they don't have what it takes, when in reality they merely need to practice. Reading and writing, though related, aren't twins. It takes a whole new set of study to become proficient as a writer. But if that's what you want, it's worth the work.

There were plenty of exterior obstacles, but my biggest has always been myself. I've always known deep down that I wanted to write professionally, but I formerly believed it to be such an unreal ambition that for years I didn't treat it with the respect it needed. I pursued other careers and other goals because it seemed so unattainable. I sabotaged myself by thinking that I would only be a real writer if I published something and then looked at everything I published with contempt for one ill-formed reason or another.

I ran myself off an anxiety cliff worrying about whether or not what I did was good enough. And then, in a phase of self-care, I told myself I would quit writing. And I did; I quit pursuing a writing career for three years. And what I found was that I still wrote. I wrote poems that didn't seem like poems, essays that didn't seem like essays, and eventually started a book that wasn't a book. The difference was that I expected nothing out of any of it. I did it because I enjoyed it. I wasn't sharing the work with anyone; I had no intentions of publishing any of it. It was only after three years of a monkish realignment of my perspective that I was able to gently tiptoe myself back into critique group, public readings, and eventually into the submission process.

LANGLEY:

How do you feel social media has changed things for authors?

NEUGEBAUER:

As with almost all new technologies, for better and for worse. The opportunities are endless: marketing, networking, connecting, learning, teaching, selling, publishing, and on and on. But of course those things can all also be distractions and time-drains. Learning how to effectively utilize social media takes a lot of time and is a moving target. There's also a potentially scary-ugly side to social media; we've seen authors mocked and torn down and careers destroyed. Ultimately, social media means more accessibility for—and to—authors, which can be beneficial and risky in equal measure. I have a love/hate relationship with social media.

BUBERT:

If you are someone who wants to connect with readers and is comfortable with self-promotion (and can do it well), social media is a godsend when you're feeling pretty low but can receive feedback from a stranger that makes your heart pitter-patter and help you remember that you're not that awful after all. Of course, this siren song of feedback can also turn into a feedback loop that your lizard brain isn't equipped to handle,

BUBERT:

and the next thing you know it's weeks later and you've made a lot of tweets and Instagram posts but haven't started on your book.

LANGLEY:

What do you feel are the advantages of online publishing versus traditional publishing?

AUGUST:

Complete creative control—you own every word in your work, and only you can make the decision to cut, keep, or change the copy. Money—you set your own price and your own royalties, plus you get paid on a regular basis (monthly vs. quarterly or every six months). Flexible timeline—if something happens to interrupt your work schedule and you have to push your book launch back a week or month or quarter, you can do that. You are not busting a publisher's timeline (thereby gaining an unreliable reputation with them).

LINTON:

The most obvious advantage of online publishing is the ease with which it can be done. If you have a completed manuscript, you're a button press away from publication. With traditional publishing, you have to first survive the slush piles, rising to the top among the sea of other hopeful authors. Once selected by an agent or editor, you then face rewrites, content edits, marketing team approval, and finally finding a slot on their often-packed publishing schedule. A process that takes minutes could take years on the trad pub end.

With a smaller overhead, fewer commitments to massive distribution channels and the bloated, and increasingly expensive, paper book trade, you won't need to sell thousands or tens of thousands of copies to be a "success." You can get

LINTON:

by with much smaller profits simply because you aren't trying to support a massive machine that constantly churns out more books and relies heavily on blockbuster sales to even be viable. Only you decide when a book has failed.

LANGLEY:

What do you feel are the disadvantages of online publishing versus traditional publishing?

AUGUST:

Lack of editing—editing is so important, and it needs to be done by a professional, someone you must pay, someone who doesn't have a dog in your race. A good editor will help you round out your books, finding the issues you may not see, or suggesting changes that only strengthen your book.

Also, it's all on you to market your book. Besides finding the time to do a book launch, you've also got to find avenues to launch it, and they continually change.

HAMMOND:

The high volume of crap novels you're competing against.

LINTON:

One of the most obvious disadvantages of online publishing is the ease with which it can be done. . . . That completed manuscript you are one finger-twitch away from showing off to the entire world, are you sure it's complete? Has it received a thorough, paid, and professional edit? A proofread? Has it even been put through the authorial paces of multiple, gut-wrenching drafts? Did you pay a pro to design your cover? Have you gotten feedback from beta readers and fans of the genre or sent Advance Reader Copies to well-regarded critics and bloggers?

LINTON:

Do you have a marketing plan in place and a solid launch strategy? Nine out of ten times, the answer self-publishers give to the majority of these questions is "no," and this is far from an exhaustive list. But you need every single box checked before you hit PUBLISH if you plan to succeed.

LANGLEY:

What tips might you recommend to newcomers looking to get into the business?

AUGUST:

Write regularly. Guard your writing time. Treat it like a job and make sure those around you do the same. And don't put your writing on the back burner because you feel guilty about closeting yourself away for an hour or two a few times a week. Find a critique group or critique partners. For partners, make sure you can work together. Don't be afraid to walk away from a partnership that doesn't work or becomes toxic. For a critique group, look for something that is convenient for you and that you will attend regularly. Even if you don't have work to bring in, you can offer your own advice and usually learn from the advice other members are giving to the works being read.

Join a craft organization if possible. There are many writers' associations such as the Romance Writers of America, Fantasy & Science Fiction Writers, Novelists Inc., Sisters in Crime, Horror Writers Association, and plenty more. Find a professional group, attend their lectures, seminars, and conferences. Join in on chat loops and e-mail exchanges. Absorb everything you can from these people, because they have a lot of wisdom to impart.

Don't give up. Your first book might not work out (mine is hiding in an impenetrable safe protected by a black mamba and Pee Wee Herman), but each project brings about better skills, better writing.

Define your own version of success. Publishing is not a one-size-fits-all industry. What someone else considers the barometer of success might not be what you consider it to be. Find your own path.

Learn to listen to and implement feedback. Research your genre, the industry, and how to be professional in this field. Be persistent in your submissions, querying, etc. Don't give up, but don't get stuck on any one project, either. Keep producing, because the more you produce, the better it will get. Go to some events when you're new: conferences, meetings, workshops, whatever you can find. You don't have to hit the pricey ones; some are even free or offer scholarships. You'll learn a lot and meet good people, so you won't be alone in this difficult journey. (Bonus: Writers are *the best* people.) And definitely don't quit your day job without some kind of backup finance in place; everything in publishing takes ten times longer than you think it should. On that note, work toward patience and enjoy the ride, because it will be a long one, but it will also be crazy fun.

BUBERT:

Start slow with the right perspective. You are very likely *not* going to become a billionaire by being a writer of fiction. You are probably not even going to make a living wage without some other kind of supplement like a part-time job, speaking engagements, or other paid writing along the lines of marketing copy or nonfiction freelance work. And if you do manage to make a living wage, it is going to take some time. Like years, maybe even decades. If you start the work in order to fund your escape from the world of working stiffs, you're very likely not going to like what you write (or what you find yourself agreeing to write).

RICHARDS:

Spend time with other writers, but don't spend all your time with just writers. You need a non-writing community to keep you balanced . . . and to get ideas you'll never get if you only hang around with other writers.

Don't spend much time on studying the business of writing until you've spent a lot of time studying the craft of writing. Have two or three books under your belt before you become too involved in the business side of things, because it changes so rapidly that what you learn today could be obsolete by the time you're ready to use it.

Don't sit too long. Write on a timer and take plenty of breaks so you don't destroy your circulation or give yourself a too-broad backside. Too late for me, but save yourself!

Love the process or quit. There are so many things to do in the world. You should only sit alone in a room making up stories if you truly enjoy it. Otherwise, get out there and find the thing you truly love to do.

Don't wait. If you want to write, start now, even if it's only for a few minutes a day.

Don't. No, seriously. There are some critical supply-and-demand issues. With online publishing's explosion, those issues have gone from bad to worse. Likely, there aren't any more writers in the world since the gates came crashing down, but there is no control on the flow. In truth, it's a wonderful curse. At no point in history has it been easier for a person to take their lovingly crafted novel and put it in front of the teeming masses. But at no point in history has it been easier for the unprepared, the hopelessly untalented, to clog the works with their monkey-at-a-typewriter drivel.

To be clear, though—one person's monkey at a typewriter is another person's Shakespeare.

So if you're dead set on the idea of being an underpaid, overworked seller of lies in a world already full of half-truths and nothing I say will dissuade you, then you've probably got the right attitude to succeed.

STARTING POINT: SELF-PUBLISHED WRITING

Becoming a self-published writer requires a writer to be all things in fostering the growth of their career: creator, editor, promoter, market analyst, web designer, tinker, tailor, soldier, spy. It's a road that starts smooth and gets rockier as you continue driving, requiring powerful determination if you expect your book to do anything other than clog up your hard drive.

THE SELF-PUBLISHING COMPETITION IS VAST, WEIRD, AND GENERALLY NOT VERY GOOD

Since anyone can self-publish their books, *everyone* is self-publishing. There's an absolute mountain of garbage out there dragging down the overall quality of works to be found in self-publishing. For every competently assembled best-seller—like H. M. Ward's Damaged series or Amanda Hocking's Trylle Trilogy—out there, you get a thousand overly ambitious genre romps with titles like *Salandris Reborn: Book One of the DarkSyde Chronicles: A Revengeance Best Served Cold* or boring rehashes of the author's family history with generic titles like *Jack's Journey*.

To help beat the competition, you'll want to out-professional them. This also means taking a critical eye to your work where others don't. If you read most self-pubs, it's clear that the only people who've read the work were the author, their close relations, and maybe an editor who has a financial investment in trying to get along with the author and not tell them that their 900-page magnum opus about a guy who discovers he's a blood descendant of Sonic the Hedgehog is, in fact, garbage. Find some good critique partners and have them check out your work before you put it out to the world; not only will it help you find your weaknesses, but critiquing the work of other interested writers will also help hone your skills.

Out-professionaling the competition also means paying some professionals to help get your book in good shape. Firstly, you'll likely want an editor. Search long and hard to find someone good, someone whose interest is in helping you make the best book, not in making you a happy panda so you'll keep throwing them business even if your book has gargantuan flaws in it. Secondly, unless you have extensive knowledge in graphic design, you should probably fork over the bucks to get a professional to make a cover for you.

Despite the adage telling them not to, people can and should judge a book by its cover; after all, it's the first thing we see of the work, and if that cover stinks it implies incompetence on the part of the author.

STAY CURRENT ON SELF-PUBLISHING STRATEGIES

The zeitgeist of self-publishing strategies is a capricious spirit. The strategies that are cutting-edge ideas on how to market your book could become the go-to strategy of next week, the over-saturated strategy of the next, and a waste of time after that. To market your book well, you'll need to stay on the cutting edge of how people are marketing their work, which means talking to others, watching trends, subscribing to newsletters, and doing as much research as you can.

"Every marketing strategy has a life cycle, and, from what I can tell, those life cycles keep getting shorter and shorter. I watched a proven strategy degrade over six months as a host of 'authorpreneurs' selling marketing classes singlehandedly flooded the space with new students. [The strategy] was long in the tooth already (marketing funnels that offer free books, collect e-mails, and send readers through a drip marketing campaign designed to encourage engagement and weed out non-fans). It's been a go-to for about three years now, and that's pushing the shelf life pretty far.

The real thing is that you have to be flexible and adjust to whatever comes along, and find some other way to make direct contact with your readers and not rely on Amazon or some third party to contact them for you."

—Russ Linton, author

DIGITAL PUBLISHING WILL PROBABLY BE WHERE YOU MAKE MOST OF YOUR MONEY

The price point on digital publishing, for both you and the consumer, is considerably lower than that of physical publishing, so most of your income is probably going to come through electronic sales. People are a lot more willing to experiment with new authors when their books cost ten bucks or less.

NICHE NOVELLAS AND SHORT STORIES ARE A BIG MARKET
Oddly enough, while traditional publishing doesn't offer much of a market for niche novellas and short stories, the low cost of entry and quick read time of these works make them perfect for an online market—doubly so if your work could even tangentially be qualified as niche erotica.

WORDS FROM WORKING NERDS

The man, the myth, the legend: **Chuck Tingle**. Who is this mysterious Dr. Tingle, whose works of erotic satire blend surreal humor, biting wit, and hardcore gay sex? No one knows for sure. His works include *Pounded in the Butt by My Own Butt, Buttception: A Butt within a Butt within a Butt, Pounded in the Pound: Turned Gay by the Socioeconomic Implications of Great Britain Leaving the European Union*, and the Hugo award–nominated *Space Raptor Butt Invasion*. Thanks to his impressive bibliography and strong online presence, Dr. Tingle has appeared on comedy shows and television and has earned the elusive position of successful, sought-after online author. In a rare interview with the elusive author, I got him to open up in his own special, grammatically unique way about who he is and how he writes.

How would you describe yourself?

hello name is doctor chuck tingle and i am known as the worlds greatest author but also as a proud dad of my handsome son (name of jon) also as big time man about town in billings this is a place in montana so that is my way thanks

What is your workday routine?

well first things first gotta wake up and have some spaghetti maybe a chocolate milk then i get out of bed and start MORNING MEDITATION this is where i think about my way and the way of others and maybe even the way of the world. then i think 'HOW CAN I PROVE LOVE TODAY?' this can seem like a really big time question but when you think about it it is not that way because we can ALL PROVE LOVE IN OUR OWN WAY. so i would say most buckaroos should start there day like this and think about how they can make a positive way for their timeline (in their own unique way that we all have) so maybe they could trot to the store and get a present for their bud or maybe they could let someone else go in the door before them or maybe they could donate money to a nice charity these are all great ways to prove love is real for all who kiss

Where do you get your ideas for your writing, and how do you keep from procrastinating?

most ideas come from meditating just thinking on the world. sometimes when i am watching news with son jon and KLOWY i see a story and think 'this is a perfect tingler' so then i will start writing like that it all depends i think best advice is listen to your timeline it will have a flow and it will point you in the direction of ideas you don't have to fight it

well for man name of chuck there is opposite problem to say HOW THE HECK DO YOU STRIKE BACK (LIKE A STARS WAR HAHAHAHAHAHAHAHAHAHA) when you WRITE TO MUCH? this is my problem as a working man sometimes i write so dang much my brain starts to hurt and makes me feel like a hog in a hog bin. so procrastination is not my enemy most of the time it is my bud. so i like to fix this way by walking to the park or talking to my son jon (he is handsome). I am sorry that this is opposite answer to question

Who or what are your inspirations?

STEVES KING is a real big timer i like to enjoy his way mostly storys like THATS A DANG BIG DOG or GET THESE BONES OUT OF THE LAKE YOU DUMMY or JACKS BACK: MY DAD IN THE MAZE so these are some of my favorites also R L STIME has many good books mostly where you think its a monster but then its actually a cat and you think wow what a relief but then later its actually a monster

In today's busy society, full of living objects and bigfoot pirate ghosts, how do you find the time to balance your schedule of writing, social media, and spaghetti?

i am working a lot it is nice when jon and KLOWY go to work because then i get the house to myself and i can get a lot done so that is mostly how i spend my time. it is easy because i get to decide 'oh i would like to go do this now because this is my butts heart' and then i go and make my way through the day. so because i am on my own schedule as a buckaroo that part is pretty easy no problem so far unless i slip into another timeline but that is a tale for another day buster

Your works feature many recurring elements—meta self-awareness, living objects, bigfoots, void crabs, etc. What is it about these elements that drew you to using them as writing motifs?

well after traveling through many layers of THE TINGLEVERSE i have learned that meta power is very good energy source not as good as love but it can work sometimes if you need to move through layers. so when i explore timelines i remember that way and i think this influences my writing as a buckaroo.

Do you feel your approach to writing has changed over time?

now when i write i do not need to hide my words under the floor like when i was in HOME OF TRUTH UTAH those were sad days ahead mostly and then when there was the big fire it was also a sad day but then i got to LEAVE THE HECK OUTTA DODGE so then i left and then son jon entered this timeline and that made love real and i am so happy about this way and so proud of my son he is the coolest guy on the block. so my writing has changed because now i do not need to hide it under the floor son jon and sam rand help me make it into the Internet

You project encouragement and positivity through your online presence. How do you keep such positivity in the face of negativity and void crabs?

as a doctor i have seen maybe buckaroos who battle with GVM (GREATEST VOID MADNESS) and that is NOT A FUN WAY so i understand how important it is to avoid this way at all costs sometimes it is hard when i hear the lonesome train or if i stare between layers of the tingleverse to long but mostly it is okay. so then you think 'what am i thankful for in this world?' and there is just so dang much i am so lucky and grateful so i think that makes proving love easy

What tips might you recommend to newcomers looking to get into writing and online publishing?

number one tips is to prove love is real with every word you write dont need to know anything other than that

BE PREPARED TO RUTHLESSLY, ENDLESSLY SELF-PROMOTE

If there's only one thing you learn from Chuck Tingle or any other successful online publisher, it's that you will need to be persistent in your self-promotion because no one else is going to do it for you.

You will, however, drive friends, families, and acquaintances away if all you talk about is your book on your personal Facebook account. So try to focus most of your self-promotion on more impersonal social networks like Twitter or Instagram, and also consider creating alternate social network accounts specifically for your author stuff.

BE PREPARED TO GET PRETTY BUSINESS-Y ABOUT IT

Self-publishing is a business, which means there will be many not-so-creative things you'll need to do to be successful—tracking things like income, advertising returns, costs, etc. If you've got some extra money lying around, you can always pay someone else to do the more business-oriented stuff, but with that you decrease the odds of turning a profit since you're chipping away at one of the most clear-cut advantages of self-publishing—the low cost of entry.

IF YOU WANT PEOPLE TO REVIEW YOUR BOOK, YOU'LL HAVE TO GO OUT AND WRANGLE 'EM

It's *hard* to get people to review self-pubs, and that's because most self-pubbed books suck a mean pile of butts. This is where having established book/geek/business connections comes in handy, as it's a lot easier to get someone you know to do a quick read and write-up of your book than it is a stranger.

MAKE SURE YOUR BOOK READS WELL DIGITALLY AND YOUR COVER LOOKS GOOD SMALL

People browse and read on a zillion different kinds of devices, and while it's impossible to make 100 percent sure your work looks good on every single kind of device, you can still check the basic three: computer screen, phone, and tablet. Before you send your work off with the okay to go to print (physically *or* digitally), double-check to see if it looks okay at different sizes and resolutions.

BE WARY OF SCAMS AND BAD INVESTMENTS

With so many people eager to self-publish, there's a whole metropolis of cottage industries around it, with companies offering editing services, creative writing courses, marketing plans, etc. Some are legit, offering the services you need at a semi-reasonable price. Others are not, and want to rip your head from your spine and suck every cent from your brainpan. Even the most legitimate, non-head-ripping businesses, however, can make no guarantee that spending money will lead to a profit. Yes, if you want to be taken seriously you'll need a professional cover for your book and a professional editor to ensure the thing makes sense, but there's no easy way to get returns on your investment. You may spend a lot of money without seeing a lot of return (for a while).

DON'T BE HEARTBROKEN IF YOUR FIRST (OR SECOND, OR THIRD) BOOK DOESN'T SELL WELL

Whether you're publishing through traditional venues or self-publishing, the fact remains that your book simply may not sell very well. It's not a condemnation of your skill as a writer nor your choice of topic. Sometimes you have the right skills for the right story at the wrong time, and that's the way it is. To prevent yourself from obsessing too heavily over your previous works, the best thing you can do is to *keep writing*. Work on your next book, get it ready to get out there. Every additional book increases the sales of your other books, because when someone stumbles onto your work and likes it, they're more likely to buy other books you've written.

RESEARCH THE PUBLISHING PLATFORMS AND LEARN WHICH ONE IS RIGHT FOR YOU

IngramSpark®, Smashwords, Draft2Digital®, and Amazon's CreateSpace® each have their own advantages and disadvantages when it comes to publishing your novel. With each, you will find rabid fans who think you'd be a fool to go elsewhere and detractors who will curse your name for even considering the service. So how do you decide? As with any important decision, you do your research. Talk to people, google around, check the reviews. Get the facts about your top contenders so you can come to an educated decision.

BE BRUTAL IN YOUR EFFORTS TO BECOME A BETTER WRITER AND AVOID THE COMMON SINS OF THE SELF-PUBLISHED NOVEL

As a self-published author, the main person focusing on making your writing better is going to be *you*. This requires a self-critical eye that doesn't shy away from the blinding truth: sometimes, what you've written isn't as good as you think it is.

You see, I've read a *lot* of self-published novels. Some are good. Most are not. What's curious about them is that, despite the fact that the bad novels each have their own special kinds of badness to them, some of the same mistakes cropped up over and over again. Here are some tips all writers should know, and all self-publishing writers should know twice.

KNOW WHEN TO START YOUR NOVEL

Backstory is important, yes, but *story* is more important. Most self-pub novels should start about fifty pages later than they do and spend way too much time establishing backstory without giving any sense that there's a story coming.

DON'T BE PRECIOUS WITH YOUR PROTAGONIST

Your protagonist should go through hell to get where they need to be. Too many self-pubs treat their heroes with kid gloves because the author loves them too much. Squeeze that love from your heart and replace it with something cold and mechanized so you can do what needs to be done to make a good story.

USE THE MEDIUM TO EVOKE THE SENSES

Books can make you *feel* sensations in a way other media can't. Don't just write a scene as "Establishing Shot, Dialogue, Character Action, Dialogue, Repeat." Throw in some other senses—smell, feel, taste, touch, balance, fashion—to ground the reader.

A PROLOGUE IS NOT JUST THE FIRST CHAPTER

A prologue is an opening image, often of something very different from the main story or far back from where the story begins. The prologue primes the reader on what kind of story they're in for, while also establishing themes and ideas.

DON'T OPEN WITH YOUR MAIN CHARACTER WAKING UP OR HAVING A SYMBOLIC DREAM

Of the self-published books I read, nearly a third of them opened with the main character waking up and/or having a dream. It's a horribly overused cliché. Be better than that.

FIND THE THROUGHLINE

What is your book about? What's the main story, the *theme?* If you stumble trying to answer this, take some time to figure out the answer. If you don't know exactly what your book is about, how the hell is the audience going to know?

WHEN YOU FIRST DESCRIBE A WOMAN, DON'T LET THE FIRST THING YOU DESCRIBE ABOUT HER BE HOW PRETTY SHE IS OR ISN'T

Far, *far* too many books (and movie scripts, and comic book scripts . . .) first describe the principal women of the story in terms of how gorgeous they are (or are not). Female characters need *character* descriptions, not lyrics from a Sir Mix-a-Lot song.

DON'T WRITE STEREOTYPES

Black characters shouldn't just sit around saying things like "Dayum!" or "You go, girl!" Hispanic characters shouldn't just be maids with broken English. Asian characters shouldn't just be obsessed with honor. Women, people of color, people in the LGBTQ community, *all* sorts of people are just that—people. Human beings are complex; reflect that complexity with writing that transcends mere stereotypes.

FIGURE OUT WHO YOUR MAIN CHARACTER IS

So, so many bad self-pubs don't seem to know who their main character is, even in books that are named after a single character! They just jump from person to person, hoping to feel epic instead of meandering. Similarly, your antagonist probably shouldn't get as many chapters devoted to their POV as your main character. The antagonist is there to push back against the protagonist, not to fill time when you don't have enough for your hero to do.

MAINTAIN MOMENTUM

Slow stories are fine. Slow stories will still have a momentum to them, letting the audience know they're moving forward, moving toward a satisfying finish. Bad stories will wander and lose focus.

SHOW, DON'T TELL!

There's a reason every writing book in the world beats you over the head with this idea—too many writers *tell* you feelings, reactions, and motivations instead of showing them. It's bad writing and merits a bottom-stinging spanking.

WE STAND TOGETHER AS NERDS

Though I make my living as an author, blogger, actor, panelist, and occasional Tommy Wiseau impersonator, my story is but one of many. The knowledge contained in this book is a group effort, drawing from the collective mastery of every professional nerd I've been lucky enough to be friends with, interview, or research.

I consider myself extremely, mind-*bogglingly* fortunate to be what some would call a professional nerd, but I do so with the knowledge that this wasn't a career that appeared instantaneously for me. I've spent an unbelievable amount of time at the keyboard, clacking away in the hopes that each thing I write might be a little better than the last. I've spent countless hours at conventions meeting with people, planning and participating in panels, grumbling through airport security, chugging orange juice to recover from the convention-related illnesses I got from shaking too many hands and being coughed on too many times. I've been frustrated by projects that wouldn't come together no matter how hard I hammered them, by jobs that fell through before they even began, by unpaid work that was so much harder than the work that actually *was* paying me, by rejection after rejection after rejection.

So why did I keep going? Why do *we* keep going?

Passion. We nerds are defined by our passions; they are our fuel and fire. Whether we're passionate about pop culture because we find our flow in hanging with our friends and contemplating a good story, whether we're passionate about crafting because the place we feel most at home is wherever the dust and tools are, whether we're passionate about writing because our minds burn with the heat of words that must be placed on the page lest they incinerate us, we nerds are gifted and cursed to have a roaring inferno within that permeates the core of our being.

It will be your pleasure and responsibility to make the world a warmer place with your passion. Be kind, be creative, be fearless in your expression and merciless in pursuit of your flow. Join with others, be supportive of them, and let them be supportive of you.

A nerdy life spent with good people and good work is a nerdy life worth living indeed.

ACKNOWLEDGMENTS

Thank you to my parents, Travis and Rebecca, who raised me in a nurturing, awesomely nerdy environment and always encouraged me to find my flow. Thank you to my brother, Nicholas, for being a creative, hilarious partner in crime. Thanks to Katrina for bravely battling side by side with me in this crazy campaign we call life, always ready to block its fireballs and slay its goblins. Thanks to Spencer, whose impending birth helped me get this book done on time.

Thank you to my family-not-by-blood: Marko Head, Renee Couey, Sarah "Fiz" Fuller, Stephen Huckabee, Tim Yarbrough, and Carly Cate. You're each a far better friend than I deserve, and I heart-emoji the hell out of you forevz.

Thank you to my writer friends, without whom my writing skills would be at the same level as that of a moldy orange in a paper sack: Sam Cumings, Jennifer August, Razaq Duradoye, Molly Jessup, Annie Neugebauer, Febe Moss, Ben Inn, Lisa Bubert, Courtney Castner, Cassie Whitmire, Laura Maisano, Laurie Brown, Nush Forte, Richard-Michael Calzada, Clay Brant, Kim Adelaar, Lori Burkheart, Regina Richards, Dan Hammond, Russ Linton, and every other member of the Denton Writer's Critique Group.

Thank you to the other working nerds who kindly allowed me to interview them about what it's like to fight the good fight of trying to earn a nerdy living: April Gloria, Allen Pan, Linsdsay Ellis, Bethany Claire, Bill Doran, Ginny DiGiuseppe, Janina Scarlet, Jenna Busch, Sistah K, Oh My Sophii, Justin McElroy, Ronnie Filyaw, Tony Kim, Troy Benjamin, and the unstoppable, enigmatic Chuck Tingle.

Thank you to my agent, Caitlin McDonald, whose endless knowledge and determination has helped propel my work forward. Thank you to Creees Hyunsung Lee for providing the sock-blowing-off art for the book. Thank you to the magnificent team at Sterling for putting their considerable talents toward making this book happen: Kate Zimmerman, Kayla Overbey, Phil Gaskill, and Hayley Jozwiak for editorial work; Lorie Pagnozzi and Gavin Motnyk for interior design; David Ter-Avanesyan and Susan Levitt for their work on the cover; and Ardi Alspach for publicity.

ENDNOTES

1   AmyatWired, "A DIY Data Manifesto," Wired, Feb 3, 2011, https://www.wired.com/2011/02/take-back-the-tubes/.

2   Declan McCullagh, "Blogs turn 10—who's the father?," CNET, Mar 20, 2007, https://www.cnet.com/news/blogs-turn-10-whos-the-father/.

3   Brooke Magnanti, "Dr Brooke Magnanti," accessed June 1, 2018, https://www.brookemagnanti.com/.

4   Bethany Keeley, "'Blog' of 'Unnecessary' Quotation Marks," accessed June 1, 2018, http://www.unnecessaryquotes.com/.

5   Andrew Bridgman, "7 Shows Where the Main Character is the Worst Character," CollegeHumor, June 22, 2017, https://bit.ly/2sBrpOs.

6   CH Staff, "5 Love Songs Not Actually About Love," CollegeHumor, June 20, 2017, https://bit.ly/2M2ktBv.

7   Barbara Mowat, Paul Werstine, Michael Poston, Rebecca Niles, eds., *Hamlet* (Washington: Folger Shakespeare Library, n.d.).

8   "Weekly World News," Wikipedia, accessed June 6, 2018, https://en.wikipedia.org/wiki/Weekly_World_News.

9   Jeanna Nakamura and Mihaly Csikszentmihályi, "Flow Theory and Research," *The Oxford Handbook of Positive Psychology* (2009): 195-206, doi: 10.1093/oxfordhb/9780195187243.013.0018.

10   Jake the Dog, played by John DiMaggio; Adventure Time, season 1 episode 25 "His Hero," directed by Larry Leichliter (Sept 20, 2010; Cartoon Network Studios/Fredator Studios).

11   Wil Wheaton, "You Can't Pay Your Rent with 'the Unique Platform and Reach Our Site Provides,'" Wil Wheaton dot Net, Oct 27, 2015, https://bit.ly/1PPy3GA.

12   Lesley Goldberg, "Felicia Day Sees CW Airing 'Dr. Horrible' as Big Victory for Web Series," *The Hollywood Reporter*, Oct 9, 2012, https://bit.ly/2kP5XAG.

13   Jon Marcus, "Personalized TV: Why I Made a Gay Web Series," Huffington Post, Oct 2, 2012, https://bit.ly/2JjzJln.

14   Patrick Klepek, "Who Invented Let's Play Videos?" Kotaku, May 6, 2015, https://bit.ly/2fo6O9K.

15   John Cacioppo and William Patrick, *Loneliness: Human Nature and the Need for Social Connection* (New York: W. W. Norton & Company, 2008), 5.

16   Cecilia D'Anastasio, "In the Wake of Marathon Streamer's Death, Twitch Community Discusses Healthy Streaming Practices," Kotaku, Feb 2, 2017, https://bit.ly/2LsAe3s.

17   Joe Marimo, "Dying to Stream," Medium, Feb 22, 2017, https://medium.com/the-cube/dying-to-stream-ff0ed2e3dfbb.

18   AngryJoeShow, "AJS Update! Our 2-Month Vacation 2017," YouTube video, July 14, 2017, https://www.youtube.com/watch?v=z3cYWOEp-3o.

19   Jason Schreier, "I Got Death Threats for Reporting on a Video Game Delay," Kotaku, May 31, 2016, https://bit.ly/1WvmR5J.

20   Patricia Sakar, "History of Cosplay," Geeks Media, 2016, https://geeks.media/history-of-cosplay.

21   Anne Victoria Clark, "The Rock Test: A Hack for Men Who Don't Want to be Accused of Sexual Harassment," Medium, Oct 9, 2017, https://bit.ly/2y5mbxJ.

22   Helen Christofi, "Cosplay Contest Judging Criteria," Cyrprus Comic Con, Mar 9, 2016, http://cypruscomiccon.org/cosplay-contest-judging-criteria-2/.

23   "FAQ," Hero Within, accessed June 4, 2018, https://herowithinstore.com/pages/faq.

24   Megan Graham, "Eight nerds get rich off a game where Oprah sobs into Lean Cuisine," Chicago Sun-Times, May 16, 2013, accessed via Internet Archive Wayback Machine, https://bit.ly/2M2NkFG.

25   "Bartle taxonomy of player types," Wikipedia, accessed June 6, 2018, https://en.wikipedia.org/wiki/Bartle_taxonomy_of_player_types.

26   Colin Campbell, "How a love of tabletop D&D helps video game designers tell their stories," Polygon, Dec 7, 2013, https://bit.ly/2kUprEe.

27   "Podcasting Historical Timeline and Milestones," International Podcast Day, accessed June 4, 2018, https://internationalpodcastday.com/podcasting-history/.

28   Katie Levine, "Episode 195: Nerdist Podcast: Penn Jillette," Nerdist, April 18, 2012, https://nerdist.com/nerdist-podcast-penn-jillette/.